Origin of Modern Calculating Machines

Origin of Modern Calculating Machines

A chronicle of the evolution of the
principles that form the generic
make-up of the Modern
Calculating Machine

BY
J. A. V. TURCK
Member of The Western Society of Engineers

CHICAGO, 1921
Published under the auspices of
The Western Society of Engineers

Copyright, 1921, by
J. A. V. Turck

Stone Age Calculating

Foreword

THERE is nothing romantic in figures, and the average man takes little interest in any subject pertaining to them. As a result of this antipathy, there is plenty of historic evidence of man's endeavor to minimize the hated drudgery of calculation.

While history shows that, from prehistoric man down to the present age, human ingenuity has turned to mechanical means to overcome the brain fatigue of arithmetical figuring, it is within quite recent years that he has really succeeded in devising means more rapid than the human brain.

Of this modern product little has been written, except in disconnected articles that have in no case offered a complete understanding as to who were the great benefactors of mankind that gave to the world the first concrete production of these modern principles of mechanical calculation.

The writer, believing that there are many who would be interested to know the true facts relative to this subject, has given to the public, in that which follows, a chronicle of the evolution of the principles disclosed in these modern machines, along with the proofs that form the foundation for the story in a way that all may understand.

Although the subject has been handled in a way that makes it unnecessary for the reader to be carried through a jangle of tiresome mechanical construction, the writer believes that there are many interested in the detail workings of these machines, and has for that reason provided an interesting and simple description of the working of each illustrated machine, which may be read by those who wish, or skipped over, if the reader desires, without the danger of losing knowledge of the relation of each of these machines to the Art.

Chapters

	PAGE
Foreword	1
Types of Ancient and Modern Machines	5
The Early Key-Driven Art	17
The Key-Driven Calculator	50
Early Efforts in the Recording Machine Art	79
First Practical Recorders	111
Introduction of the Modern Accounting Machine	144
The High-Speed Calculator	149
The Improved Recorder	163
The Bookkeeping and Billing Machine	174
A Closing Word	190

Illustrations

	PAGE
Frontispiece, "Stone Age Calculating"	
One of the Pascal Machines	10
Photo of Blaise Pascal	11
Parmelee Patent Drawings	16
Hill Patent Drawings	23
Chapin Patent Drawings	28
From the Stark Patent Drawings	32
From the Robjohn Patent Drawings	36
From Drawings of Bouchet Patent 314,561	40
Drawings of Spalding Patent No. 293,809	46
"Macaroni Box" Model	53
Photo of Dorr E. Felt	55
The First "Comptometer"	57
From Drawings of Felt Patent No. 371,496	58
Bill for First Manufacturing Tools of the Comptometer	68
Early Comptometer	69
Letter from Geo. W. Martin	71
Testimonial	72
Testimonial	73
Letters from Elliott and Rosecrans	74
From Drawings of Barbour Patent No. 133,188	78
From Drawings of Baldwin Patent No. 159,244	83
Baldwin Machine	83
From Drawings of Pottin Patent No. 312,014	88
From Drawings of Burroughs Patent No. 388,118	94
Photo of Wm. S. Burroughs	95
Drawings of Ludlum Patent No. 384,373	104
From Drawings of Felt Patent No. 405,024	112
Testimonial	117
Felt Recording and Listing Machine	118
From Drawings of Felt Patent No. 465,255	121
Felt Tabulator	126
One of the Early "Comptographs"	130
Photo of Gottfried Wilhelm Leibnitz	132
Leibnitz Calculator	133
From Drawings of Burroughs' Patents Nos. 504,963 and 505,078	136
Burroughs' Recorder	137
From the February 1908 Issue of Office Appliances Magazine	142
The High-Speed Calculator	148
Two Pages from Wales Adding Machine Co. Booklet	165
Moon-Hopkins Billing and Bookkeeping Machine	176
Napier's Bones	179
From Drawings of Barbour Patent No. 130,404	180
Photo of John Napier	181
From Drawings of Bollee Patent No. 556,720	186

The Modern Accounting Machine

THE term "adding machine" or "calculating machine" to most of us represents the machine we have seen in the bank. The average person is not familiar with the different types of accounting machines, to say nothing of the many uses to which they are put; but he has a vague idea that to hold any value they should produce a printed record, he doesn't know why and he hasn't stopped to reason why; but those he has seen in the bank do print, and any machine the bank uses, to his mind, must be all right.

There are, of course, people who do know the different types of accounting machines, and are familiar with their special uses, but there are very few who are familiar with the true history of the modern accounting machine.

Articles written by those not familiar with the true facts relative to the art of accounting machines have wrought confusion. Their errors have been copied and new errors added, thus increasing the confusion. Again, claims made in trade advertisements and booklets are misleading, with the result that the truth is but little known.

General knowledge lacking

These facts, and the psychological effect of seeing a certain type of machine in the bank would lead the average man to believe that the recording-adding machine was the only practical machine;

and also (as someone stated in the December, 1915, issue of the Geographic Magazine) that Burroughs was the inventor of the recording-adding machine.

Although the history of accounting machines dates way back into the tenth century, the modern accounting machines are of quite recent origin, and are especially distinguished by the presence of depressable keys. The keys in these machines act as a means of gauging the actuation which determines the value in calculation, whether the machine is key-driven or key-set with a crank or motor drive.

These modern machines, which come within the classification of key-driven and key-set, have their respective special uses.

Key-driven machine first of the modern machines

The key-driven machine, which was the first produced of these two types of modern machines, does not print, and is used for all forms of calculation, but is generally behind the scenes in the accounting rooms of all lines of business, and for that reason is not so well known as the key-set crank-operated or motor-driven machine, which is designed to print and is always in full view in the bank where it is used to print your statement of account from the vouchers you have issued.

When we stop to analyze the qualities of these two types of machines, we find that each has its place and that neither may truly serve to displace the other. The organization of each is designed with reference to the special work it was intended to do.

The calculating machine, having only to perform the work of revolving the numeral wheels in calculating addition, subtraction, multiplication and division in its many forms and combinations, may be key-driven (on account of the slight mechanical resistance met with in action), and thus, as a one-motion machine, requiring only the depression of the keys, may also be much more rapid of manipulation than the two-motion recording-adding machine which, after depressing the keys for each item, requires the secondary operation of pulling a crank forward or operating a push bar that connects the motor.

The recording-adding machine being designed to print the items and answers of addition, requires power for the printing which cannot be supplied by key depression. Thus an extra means for supplying that power must be provided in the form of a crank lever, or in the latest machines by a motor. The keys in such machines serve only as digital control to gauge the setting of mechanism which prints the items and adds them together. The secondary motion operates the mechanism to print and add and finally to clear the machine for the setting up of the next item. The recording of added columns of figures requires that the answer must always be printed. This demands special operation of devices provided for that purpose, which also adds to the time spent in the operation of such machines as compared with the key-driven calculator.

To state which of these two types of machines is the more useful would cause a shower of comment, and has nothing to do with the object of this article. Suffice it to say that where a printed record of items added together with their answer is required for filing purposes, or to bring together loose items like those in your bank statement, the recording-adding machine serves; but when rapid

Recording, the primary feature of adding machines that print

calculation in addition, multiplication, subtraction or division, or when combinations of these forms of calculation are required, the key-driven calculator is the practical machine for such work.

Although the key-driven calculator is generally not so well known, it is, as stated, the oldest of the modern accounting machines, and its usefulness places it in the accounting room, where it is ofttimes found employed by the hundreds in figuring up the day's work of accounting.

Validity and priority of invention

The purpose of this book is based wholly upon showing the validity and priority of invention which constitute true contributions to the Art of these two types of modern accounting machines; to place the facts for once and all time before the public in such a way that they may judge for themselves to whom the honor is due and thus settle the controversy that exists.

The quibbling of court contests over the terminology of claims of patents owned by the various inventors have been set aside and only the true contributions to the Art which pertain to the fundamental principles that have made the modern machines possible, are here dealt with.

The dates of patents on inoperative or impractical machines have from time to time been held up to the public as instances of priority of invention; but when the validity of these patents, as furnishing any real contributions to the Art, is questioned, they are not found to hold the theme or principle that made the modern machines possible, and as inventions, fade into obscurity.

The Art of either the calculating machine or the adding-recording machine is not new; it is, as a matter of fact, very old. As before stated, the Art

Figure 1

Figure 2

One of the Pascal Machines

of "accounting machine" dates back to the tenth century, but the first authentic evidence of a working machine is extant in models made by Pascal in 1642 (see illustration).

THE PASCAL MACHINE

Referring to the illustration, Fig. 1, of Pascal's machine on the opposite page, it will be noted that there are a series of square openings in the top of the casing; under these openings are drums, each numbered on its cylindrical surface.

As the machine illustrated was made to figure English currency, the two right-hand wheels are numbered for pence and shillings, while the six wheels to the left are numbered from 1 to 9 and 0 for pounds.

Description of Pascal's invention

The pounds register-drums, or numeral wheels, are each operated by a train of gearing connecting them with a ten-armed turnstile wheel which form the hub and spokes of what appears to be a series of wheels on the top of the casing. While the spokes and hub are movable, the rims of these wheels are stationary and are numbered from 1 to 9 and 0.

The geared relation between the turnstile wheels and the numeral wheels is such that rotating a turnstile will give like rotation to its numeral wheel.

Assuming that the numeral wheel of any one of the different orders registered 0 through its sight opening and the turnstile of the same order was moved one spoke of a rotation, it would move the wheel so that the 0 would disappear and the figure 1 would appear; now if we should move the same turnstile three more spokes the numeral wheel

Blaise Pascal

would move likewise three spaces and the 4 would appear.

A stop in the form of a finger reaching over the spokes is provided to stop the turnstile at the right point so that the figures on the numeral wheels may register properly with the sight openings in the casing.

Constructional features of the Pascal machine

The figures on the wheel rims fast to the casing are arranged anti-clockwise to register with the space between the spokes, the 0 registering with the first space, the 1 with the second space and so on around the wheel. Thus by use of the finger or a stylo inserted in a space opposite the number to be added, the operator may move the spoked wheel or turnstile clockwise until stopped by the stop finger. By repeated selection and operation for each figure to be added, the wheels will be revolved through their cycles of rotation caused by the accumulation.

As the numeral wheels complete each rotation the 0 will appear, so that a registration of the tens must be made. Pascal provided for the accumulation of the tens by automatically turning the wheel of next higher order one point through the action of the lower wheel.

The novel means employed for this transfer of the tens consisted of a one-step ratchet device operated by a pin in the train of gearing connected with the lower numeral wheel, which, as the lower wheel passed from 9 to 0, forced the lever to which the ratchet pawl was attached in a direction to cause the gearing of the higher numeral wheel to be ratcheted forward far enough to add one to the higher numeral wheel.

The direct actuation of a numbered wheel through its various degrees of rotation and the secondary feature of effecting a one-step movement to the numbered wheel of higher order (which seems to have been originated by Pascal) is the foundation on which nearly all the calculating machines have since been constructed to calculate the combinations of the Arabian numerals represented in Addition, Multiplication, Subtraction and Division.

In Fig. 2 of the illustration of Pascal's machine, the machine has been reversed, and the bottom of the casing, which is hinged, thrown back, showing the numeral wheels and gearing of the different orders and the transfer levers for the carry of the tens.

The Art of the modern machines is far removed from the older Art by its greatly increased capacity for rapid calculation which is found emanating from the provision of keys as the means of manipulation. *Increased capacity of modern calculator*

To the unsophisticated, such a simple thing as applying keys to the ancient type of calculating machines that have been made and used for centuries, would seem but a simple mechanical application that the ordinary mechanic could accomplish. But it was too great a problem for the many renowned inventors of the older Art to solve.

Even though the use of depressable keys was common to many machines, especially the piano, they knew that the organized make-up of their machines could scarcely stand, without error, the slow action received from the crank motion or other means employed as manipulating devices. To place it within the power of an operator to operate their machines at such a speed as would obtain in the sudden striking of a key would result in chaos.

Patent office a repository of ineffectual efforts

There is no room for doubt that some of these early inventors had the wish or desire to produce such a key-driven machine and may have attempted to produce one. But as they lacked the advantage of an institution like the Patent Office in which they could leave a record of their inoperative inventions, and in view of the fact that they were dependent on producing an operating machine for credit, there is no authentic proof that they made attempts in this line.

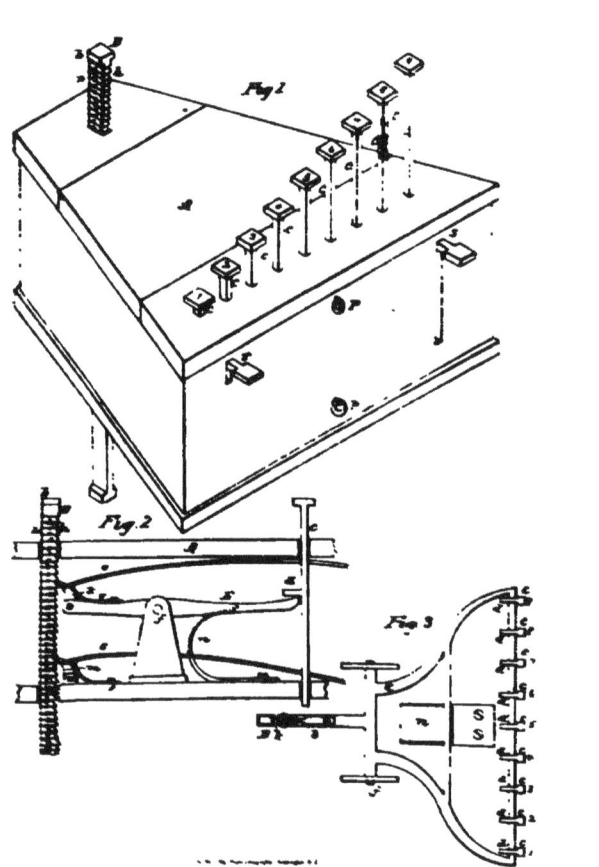

Parmelee Patent Drawings

The Early Key-Driven Art

M. LE COLONEL D'OCAGNE, Ingénieur des Ponts et Chaussées, Professeur à l'École des Ponts et Chaussées, Répétiteur à l'École Polytechnique, in his "Le Calcul simplifie," a historical review of calculating devices and machines, refers to the key-driven machine as having first made its appearance in the Schilt machine of 1851, but that the Art reached its truly practical form in America. In the latter part of his statement the professor is correct, but as to the first appearance of the key-driven machine the U. S. Patent Office records show that a patent was issued to D. D. Parmelee in 1850 for a key-driven adding machine (see illustration).

The Parmelee Machine

By referring to the illustration of the Parmelee machine reproduced from the drawings of the patent, the reader will notice that the patentee deviated from the established principle of using numeral wheels. In place of numeral wheels a long ratchet-toothed bar has been supplied, the flat faces of which are numbered progressively from the top to the bottom.

First attempt to use depressable keys for adding was made in America

As shown in Fig. 2 of these drawings, a spring-pressed ratchet pawl marked k, engages the teeth of the ratchet or numeral bar. The pawl k, is pivoted to a lever-constructed device marked E, the plan of which is shown in Fig. 3. This lever

Description of Parmelee machine

device is pivoted and operated by the keys which are provided with arms d, so arranged that when any one of the keys is depressed the arm contacts with and operates the lever device and its pawl k to ratchet the numeral bar upwards.

Another spring-pressed ratchet pawl marked m (see Fig. 2) is mounted on the bottom of the casing and serves to hold the numeral bar from returning after a key-depression.

It will be noted from Fig. 1 that the keys extend through the top of the casing in progressively varying heights. This variation is such as to allow the No. 1 key to ratchet up one tooth of the numeral bar, the No. 2 key two teeth, etc., progressively. By this method a limited column of digits could be added up by depressing the keys corresponding to the digits and the answer could be read from the lowest tooth of the numeral bar that protruded through the top of the casing.

It is evident that if the Parmelee machine was ever used to add with, the operator would have to use a pussyfoot key-stroke or the numeral bar would over-shoot and give an erroneous answer, as no provision was made to overcome the momentum that could be given the numeral bar in an adding action.

Foreign digit adders

The foreign machines of the key-driven type were made by V. Schilt, 1851; F. Arzberger, 1866; Stetner, 1882; Bagge, 1882; d'Azevedo, 1884; Petetin, 1885; Maq Meyer, 1886. These foreign machines, like that of Parmelee, according to M. le Colonel d'Ocagne, were limited to the capacity of adding a single column of digits at a time. That is, either a column of units or tens or hundreds, etc., at a time. Such machines, of course, required the adding first of all the units, and a note made of the total; then the machine must be cleared and the tens figure of the total, and hundreds, if there be one, must then be added or carried over to the tens column the same as adding single columns mentally.

Single digit adders lack capacity

On account of these machines having only a capacity for adding one order or column of digits, the unit value 9 was the greatest item that could be added at a time. Thus, if the overflow in adding the units column or any other column amounted to more than one place, it required a multiple of key-depressions to put it on the register. For example, suppose the sum of adding the units columns should be 982, it would require the depression of the 9-key ten times and then the 8-key to be struck, to put the 98 on the machine. This order of manipulation had to be repeated for each denominational column of figures.

Another method that could be used in the manipulation of these single-order or digit-adding machines was to set down the sum of each order as added with its units figure arranged relative to the order it represents the sum of, and then mentally add such sums (see example below) the same as you would set down the sums in multiplication and add them together.

Example of method that may be used with single column adder.

$$\begin{array}{r} 982 \\ 563 \\ 384 \\ 125 \\ \hline 170012 \end{array}$$

Such machines, of course, never became popular because of their limited capacity, which required many extra movements and caused mental strain without offering an increase in speed of calculation as compared with expert mental calculation. There were a number of patents issued in the United States on machines of this class which may well be named single digit-adders.

Some early U.S. patents on single-digit adding machines

The machines of this type which were patented in the United States, preceding the first practical multiple order modern machine, were patented by D. D. Parmelee, 1850; W. Robjohn, 1872; D. Carroll, 1876; Borland & Hoffman, 1878; M. Bouchet, 1883; A. Stettner, 1883; Spalding, 1884; L. M. Swem, 1885 and 1886; P. T. Lindholm, 1886; and B. F. Smith, 1887. All of these machines varied in construction but not in principle. Some were really operative and others inoperative, but all lacked what may be termed useful capacity.

To those not familiar with the technical features of the key-driven calculating machine Art, it would seem that if a machine could be made to add one column of digits, it would require no great invention or ingenuity to arrange such mechanisms in a plurality of orders. But the impossibility of effecting such a combination without exercising a high degree of invention will become evident as the reader becomes familiar with the requirements, which are best illustrated through the errors made by those who tried to produce such a machine.

As stated, the first authentic knowledge we have of an actual machine for adding is extant in models made by Pascal in 1642, which were all multiple-order machines, and the same in general as that shown in the illustration, page 10.

Calculating machines in use abroad for centuries

History shows that Europe and other foreign countries have been using calculating machines for centuries. Like that of Pascal's, they were all multiple-order machines, and, although not key-driven, they were capable of adding a number of columns or items of six to eight places at once without the extra manipulation described as necessary with single-order digit adding machines. A number of such machines were made in the United States prior to the first practical multiple-order key-driven calculator.

First key-driven machines no improvement to the Art

This fact and the fact that the only operative key-driven machines made prior to 1887 were single-digit adders are significant proof that the backward step from such multiple-order machines to a single-order key-driven machine was from the lack of some unknown mechanical functions that would make a multiple-order key-driven calculator possible. There was a reason, and a good one, that kept the inventors of these single-order key-driven machines from turning their invention into a multiple-order key-driven machine.

It is folly to think that all these inventors never had the thought or wish to produce such a machine. It is more reasonable to believe there was not one of them who did not have the wish and who did not give deep thought to the subject. There is every reason to believe that some of them tried it, but there is no doubt that if they did it was a failure, or there would be evidence of it in some form.

The Hill Machine

The U. S. Patent Office records show that one ambitious inventor, Thomas Hill, in 1857 secured a patent on a multiple-order key-driven calculating machine (see illustration), which he claimed as a new and useful invention. The Hill patent, however, was the only one of that class issued, until the first really operative modern machine was made, thirty years later, and affords a fine example by which the features that were lacking in the make-up of a really operative machine of this type may be brought out.

Description of the Hill machine

The illustrations of the Hill machine on the opposite page, reproduced from the drawings of the patent, show two numeral wheels, each having seven sets each of large and small figures running from 1 to 9 and the cipher marked on their periphery. The large sets of figures are arranged for addition or positive calculation, and the small figures are arranged the reverse for subtraction or negative calculation. The wheels are provided with means for the carry of the tens, very similar to that found in the Pascal machine. Each of the two wheels shown are provided with ratchet teeth which correspond in number with the number of figures on the wheel.

Spring-pressed, hook-shaped ratchet pawls marked b, are arranged to be in constant engagement with the numeral wheels. These pawls are each pivotally mounted in the end of the levers marked E, which are pivoted at the front end of the casing.

The levers E, are held in normal or upward position by springs f, at the front of the machine.

T. HILL.

ARITHMOMETER.

No. 18,692. Patented Nov. 24, 1857.

Hill Patent Drawings

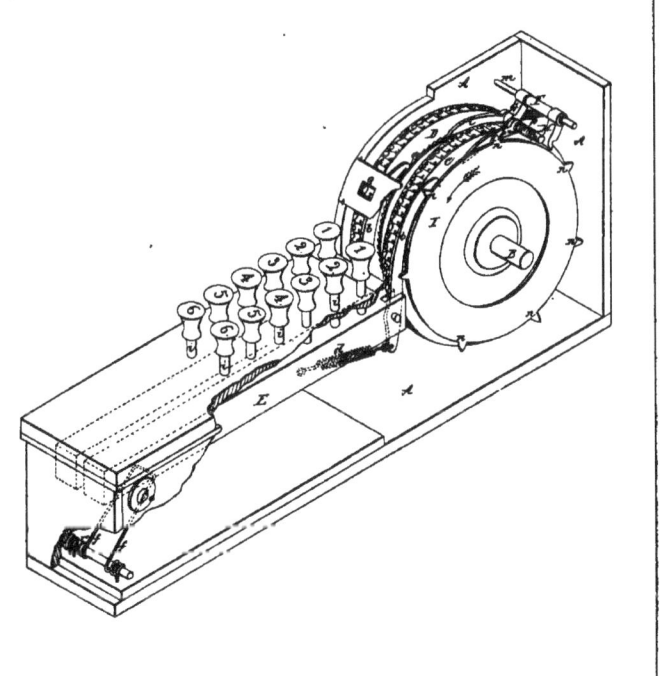

.Above each of these levers E, are a series of keys which protrude through the casing with their lower ends resting on the levers. There are but six keys shown in the drawing, but the specification claims that a complete set of nine keys may be supplied for each lever.

The arrangement and spacing of the keys are such that the greater the value of the key the nearer it is to the fulcrum or pivot of the lever E. The length of the key stem under the head or button of each key is gauged to allow depression of the key, the lever E and pawl b, far enough to cause the numeral wheel to rotate as many numeral places as the value marking on the key.

A back-stop pawl for the numeral wheels, marked p, is mounted on a cross-rod at the top of the machine. But one of these pawls are shown, the shaft and the pawl for the higher wheel being broken away to show the device for transferring the tens to the higher wheel.

The transfer device for the carry of the tens is a lever arrangement constructed from a tube F, mounted on the cross-rod m, with arms G and H. Pivoted to the arm G, is a ratchet pawl i, and attached to the pawl is a spring that serves to hold the pawl in engagement with the ratchet of the higher-order numeral wheel, and at the same time, through its attachment with the pawl, holds the lever arms G and H retracted as shown in the drawing.

As the lower-order numeral wheel passes any one of its points from 9 to 0, one of the teeth or cam lugs n, on the wheel will move the arm H, of the transfer lever forward, causing the pawl i, to move the higher-order wheel one step to register the accumulation of the tens.

The functions of the Hill mechanism would, perhaps, be practical if it were not for the physical law that "bodies set in motion tend to remain in motion."

Considerable unearned publicity has been given the Hill invention on account of the patent office model having been placed on exhibit in the National Museum at Washington. Judging from the outward appearance of this model, the arrangement of the keys in columns would seem to impart the impression that here was the foundation of the modern key-driven machine. The columnar principle used in the arrangement of the keys, however, is the only similarity.

Hill machine at National Museum

The Hill invention, moreover, was lacking in the essential feature necessary to the make-up of such a machine, a lack that for thirty years held the ancient Art against the inroads of the modern Art that finally displaced it. The feature lacking was a means for controlling the action of the mechanism under the tremendously increased speed produced by the use of depressable keys as an actuating means.

Inoperativeness of Hill machine

Hill made no provision for overcoming the lightning-speed momentum that could be given the numeral wheels in his machine through manipulation of the keys, either from direct key-action or indirectly through the carry of the tens. Imagine the sudden whirl his numeral wheel would receive on a quick depression of a key and then consider that he provided no means for stopping these wheels; it is obvious that a correct result could not be obtained by the use of such mechanism. Some idea of what would take place in the Hill machine under manipulation by an operator may be conceived from the speed attained in the operation of the keys of the up-to-date modern key-driven machine.

High speed of key drive

Operators on key-driven machines oftentimes attain a speed of 550 key strokes a minute in multiplication. Let us presume that any one of these strokes may be a depression of a nine key. The depression and return, of course, represents a full stroke, but only half of the stroke would represent the time in which the wheel acts. Thus the numeral wheel would be turned nine of its ten points of rotation in an eleven hundredth (1/1100) of a minute. That means only one-ninth of the time given to half of the key stroke, or a ninety-nine hundredth (1/9900) of a minute; a one hundred and sixty-fifth (1/165) part of a second for a carry to be effected.

Camera slow compared with carry of the lens

If you have ever watched a camera-shutter work on a twenty-fifth of a second exposure, which is the average time for a snap-shot with an ordinary camera, it will be interesting to know that these controlling devices of a key-driven machine must act in one-fifth the time in which the shutter allows the daylight to pass through the lens of the camera.

Think of it; a machine built with the idea of offering the possibility of such key manipulation and supplying nothing to overcome the tremendous momentum set up in the numeral wheels and their driving mechanism, unless perchance Hill thought the operator of his machine could, mentally, control the wheels against over-rotation.

Lack of a proper descriptive term used to refer to an object, machine, etc., oftentimes leads to the use of an erroneous term. To call the Hill inven-

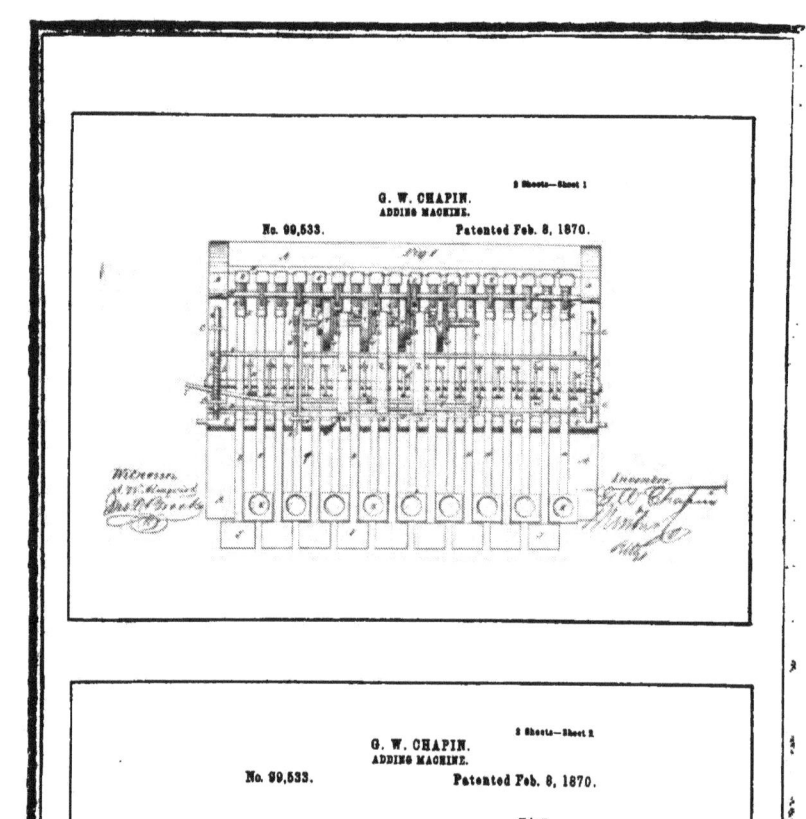

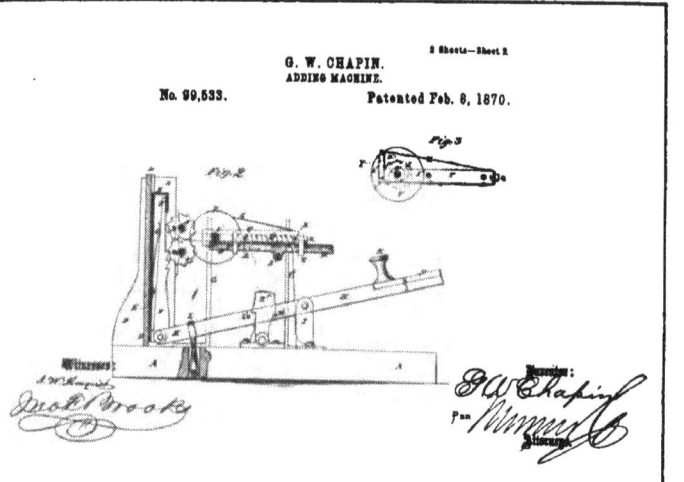

Chapin Patent Drawings

tion an adding machine is erroneous since it would not add correctly. It is as great an error as it would be to refer to the Langley aeroplane as a flying machine.

When the Wright brothers added the element that was lacking in the Langley plane, a real flying machine was produced. But without that element the Langley plane was not a flying machine. Likewise, without means for controlling the numeral wheels, the Hill invention was not an adding machine. The only term that may be correctly applied to the Hill invention is "adding mechanism," which is broad enough to cover its incompleteness. And yet many thousands of people who have seen the Hill invention at the National Museum have probably carried away the idea that the Hill invention was a perfectly good key-driven adding machine.

Hill machine merely adding mechanism, incomplete as operative machine

Lest we leave unmentioned two machines that might be misconstrued to hold some of the features of the Art, attention is called to patents issued to G. W. Chapin in 1870 (see illustration on opposite page), and A. Stark in 1884 (see illustration on page 32).

Chapin and Stark patents

CHAPIN MACHINE

Referring to the illustration reproducing the drawings of the Chapin patent, the reader will note that in Fig. 1 there are four wheels marked V. These wheels, although showing no numerals, are, according to the specification, the numeral wheels of the machine.

Description of Chapin machine

The wheels are provided with a one-step ratchet device for transferring the tens, consisting of the spring frame and pawl shown in Fig. 3, which is operated by a pin in the lower wheel.

In Fig. 1 the units and tens wheel are shown meshed with their driving gears. These gears are not numbered but are said to be fast to the shafts N and M, respectively (see Fig. 2).

Fast on the shaft M, is a series of nine ratchet-toothed gears marked O, and a like series of gears P, are fast to the shaft N. Co-acting with each of these ratchet-toothed gears is a ratchet-toothed rack F, pivoted at its lower end to a key lever H, and pressed forward into engagement with its ratchet gear by a spring G.

The key levers H, of which there are two sets, one set with the finger-pieces K and the other with the finger-pieces J, are all pivoted on the block I, and held depressed at the rear by an elastic band L. The two sets of racks F, are each provided with a number of teeth arranged progressively from one to nine, the rack connected with the No. 1 key having one ratchet tooth, the No. 2 having two teeth, etc.

Inoperativeness of Chapin machine

By this arrangement Chapin expected to add the units and tens of a column of numerical items, and then by shifting the numeral wheels and their transfer devices, which are mounted on a frame, designed for that purpose, he expected to add up the hundred and thousands of the same column of items.

It is hardly conceivable that the inventor should have overlooked the necessity of gauging the throw of the racks F, but such is the fact, as no provision is made in the drawings, neither was mention made of such means in the specification. Even a single tooth on his rack F, could, under a quick key-stroke, overthrow the numeral wheels, and the same is true of the carry transfer mechanism.

From the Stark Patent Drawings

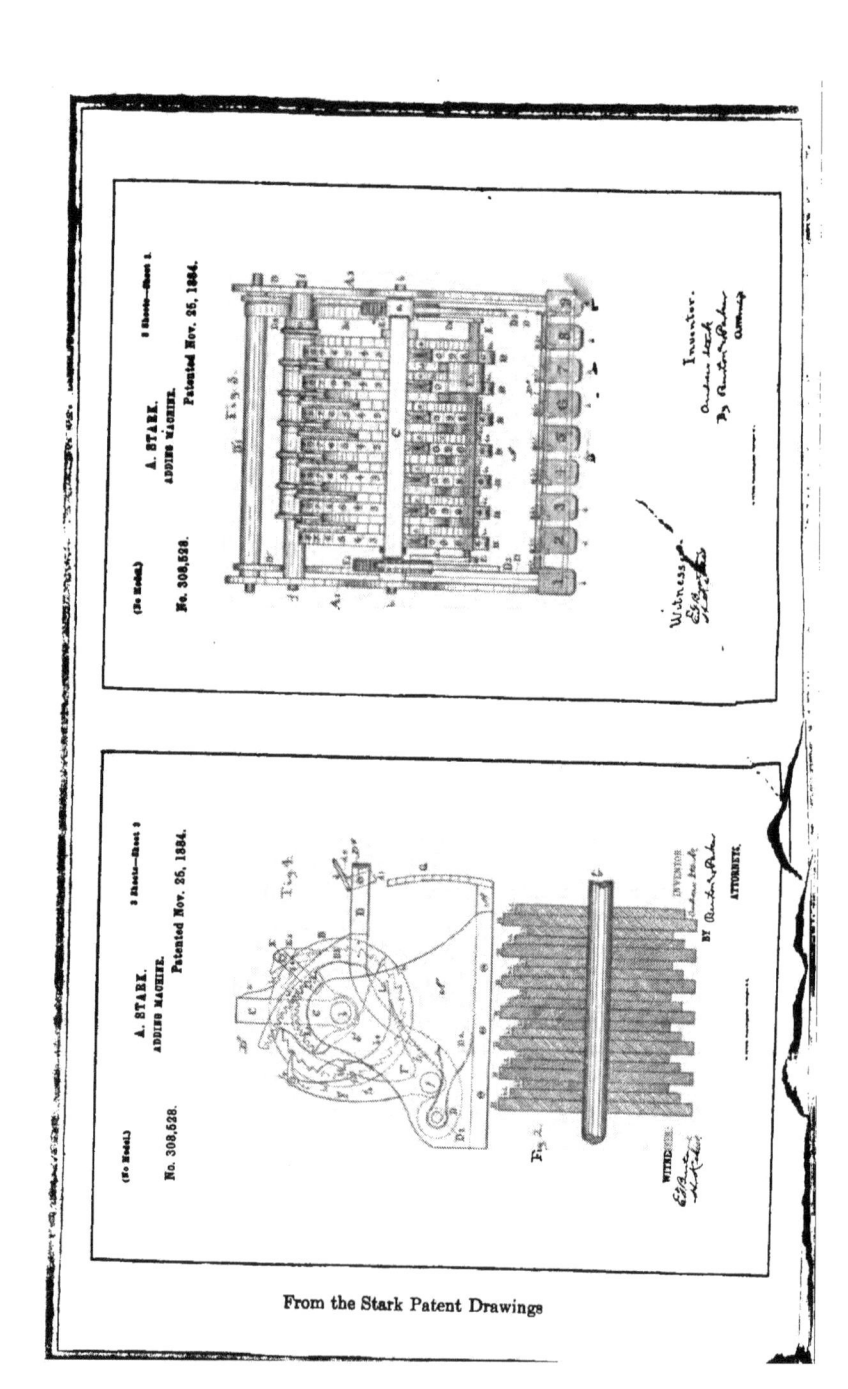

The Chapin machine, like that of Hill, was made without thought as to what would happen when a key was depressed with a quick stroke, as there was no provision for control of the numeral wheels against overthrow. As stated, the machine was designed to add two columns of digits at a time, and with an attempt to provide means to shift the accumulator mechanism, or the numeral wheels and carry-transfer devices, so that columns of items having four places could be added by such a shift. Such a machine, of course, offered less than could be found in the Hill machine, and that was nothing at all so far as a possible operative machine is concerned.

The Stark Machine

The reproduction of the patent drawings of the Stark machine illustrated on the opposite page show a series of numeral wheels, each provided with three sets of figures running from 1 to 9 and 0.

Pivotally mounted upon the axis of the numeral wheels at each end are sector gears E^1 and arms E^4, in which are pivoted a square shaft E, extended from one arm to the other across the face of the numeral wheels. The shaft E, is claimed to be held in its normal position by a spring so that a pawl, E^2, shiftably mounted on the shaft, designed to ratchet or actuate the numeral wheels forward, may engage with any one of the numeral wheel ratchets.

Description of Stark machine

A bail marked D, is pivoted to standards A^1, of the frame of the machine, and is provided with the two radial racks D^3, which mesh with the sector gears E^1. It may be conceived that the act of depressing the bail D, will cause the actuating pawl E², to operate whichever numeral wheel it engages the ratchet of.

The bail D, is held in its normal position by a spring D², and is provided with nine keys or finger pieces d, eight of which co-act with the stepped plate G, to regulate the additive degree of rotation given to the numeral wheels, while the ninth has a fixed relation with the bail and the bail itself is stopped.

The keys d, marked from 1 to 8, are pivoted to the bail in such a manner that their normal relation to the bail will allow them to pass by the steps on the stepped plate G, when the bail is depressed by the fixed No. 9 key. When, however, any one of the keys numbered from 1 to 8 is depressed, the lower end of the shank of the key will tilt rearward, and, as the bail is depressed, offers a stop against the respective step of the plate G, arranged in its path, thus stopping further action of the actuating pawl E², but offering nothing to prevent the continuation of the force of momentum set up in the numeral wheels by the key action.

There was small use in stopping the action of the pawl E², if the ratchet and numeral wheel, impelled by the pawl, could continue onward under its momentum.

The carry of the tens transfer device is of the same order as that described in the Pascal and Hill machines; that is, a one-step ratchet-motion actuated by a cam lug or pin from the lower wheel. The carry transfer device consists of the lever F, and pawl f⁴, acting on the ratchet of the upper wheel which is operated by the cam lugs b⁵, of the lower wheel acting on the arms f¹ and f³ of the lever F.

From the Robjohn Patent Drawings

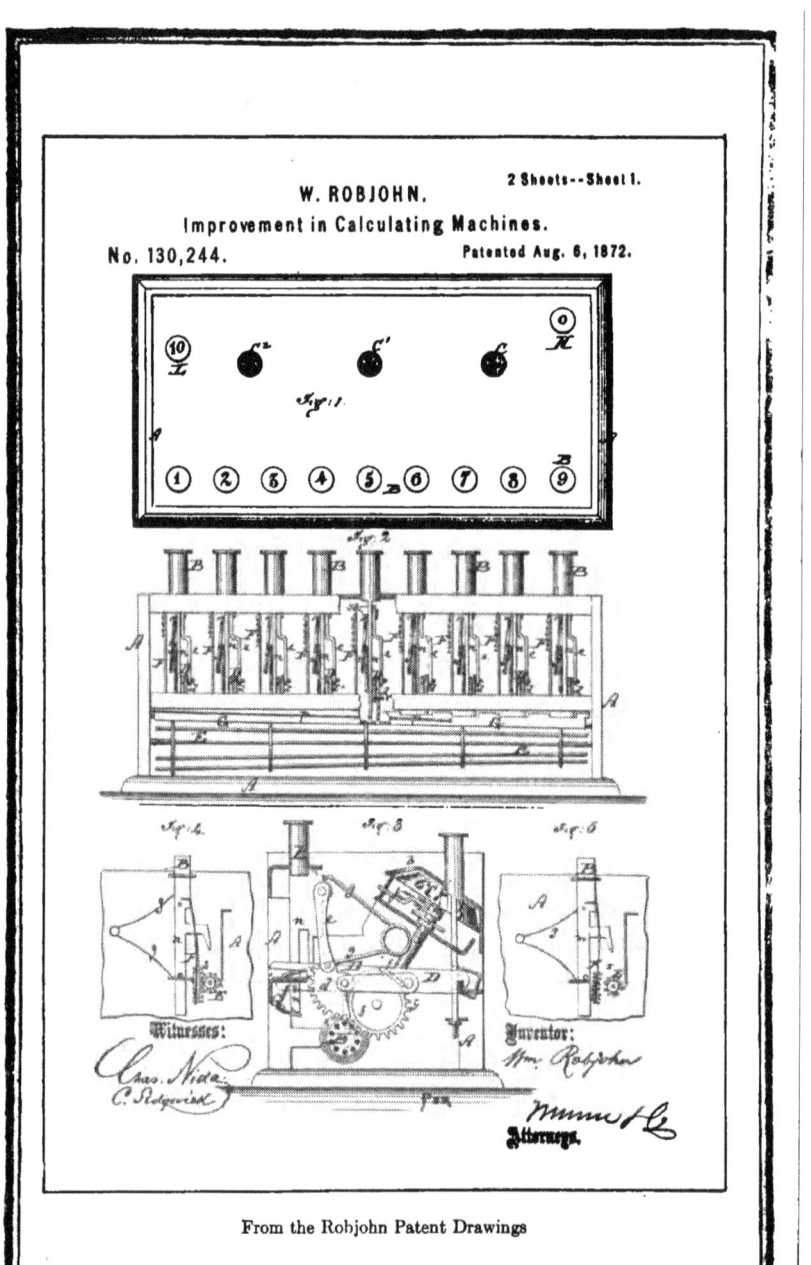

The machine shown in the Stark patent was provided with but one set of keys, but the arrangement for shifting the driving ratchet pawl E^2, from one order to another, so that the action of the keys may rotate any one of the numeral wheels, gave the machine greater capacity than the single digit adders; but as with the Chapin machine, of what use was the increase in capacity if the machine would not add correctly. That is about all that may be said of the Stark machine, for since there was no means provided by which the rotation of numeral wheels could be controlled, it was merely a device for rotating numeral wheels and was therefore lacking in the features that would give it a right to the title of an adding machine.

Inoperativeness of Stark machine

The nine-key scheme of the Stark invention, connectable to the different orders, was old, and was first disclosed in the U. S. Patent to O. L. Castle in 1857 (a machine operated by a clock-spring wound by hand), but its use in either of these machines should not be construed as holding anything in common with that found in some of the modern recording adders. The Castle machine has not been illustrated because it does not enter into the evolution of the modern machine.

Nine keys common to a plurality of orders

The ancient Art, or the Art prior to the invention of Parmelee, consisted of mechanism which could be controlled by friction devices, or Geneva gear-lock devices, that were suitable to the slow-acting type of manipulative means.

The first attempt at a positive control for a key-driven adding device is found in a patent issued to W. Robjohn in 1872 (see illustration). As will be noted, this machine was referred to in the foregoing discussion as merely a single-digit adding machine, having the capacity for adding but one column of digits at a time.

ROBJOHN MACHINE

Referring to the illustration of the patent drawings of the Robjohn machine, it will be noted that there are three sight openings in the casing through which the registration of the numeral wheels may be read. The numeral wheels, like those of all machines of this character, are connected by devices of a similar nature to those in the Hill machine for carrying the tens, one operating between the units and tens wheel and another between the tens and hundredths wheel.

Description of Robjohn machine

The units wheel shown in Fig. 3 is connected by gearing to a long pin-wheel rotor, marked E, so that any rotation of the rotor E, will give a like rotation to the units numeral wheel to which it is entrained by gearing.

To each of the nine digital keys, marked B, is attached an engaging and disengaging sector gear device, which, as shown in Fig. 3, although normally not in engagement with the rotor E, will upon depression of its attached key, engage the rotor and turn it.

A stop device is supplied for the key action, which in turn was supposed to stop the gear action; that seems rather doubtful. However, an alternative device is shown in Figs. 4 and 5, which provides what may without question be called a stop device to prevent over-rotation of the units wheel under direct key action.

It will be noted that the engaging and disengaging gear device is here shown in the form of a

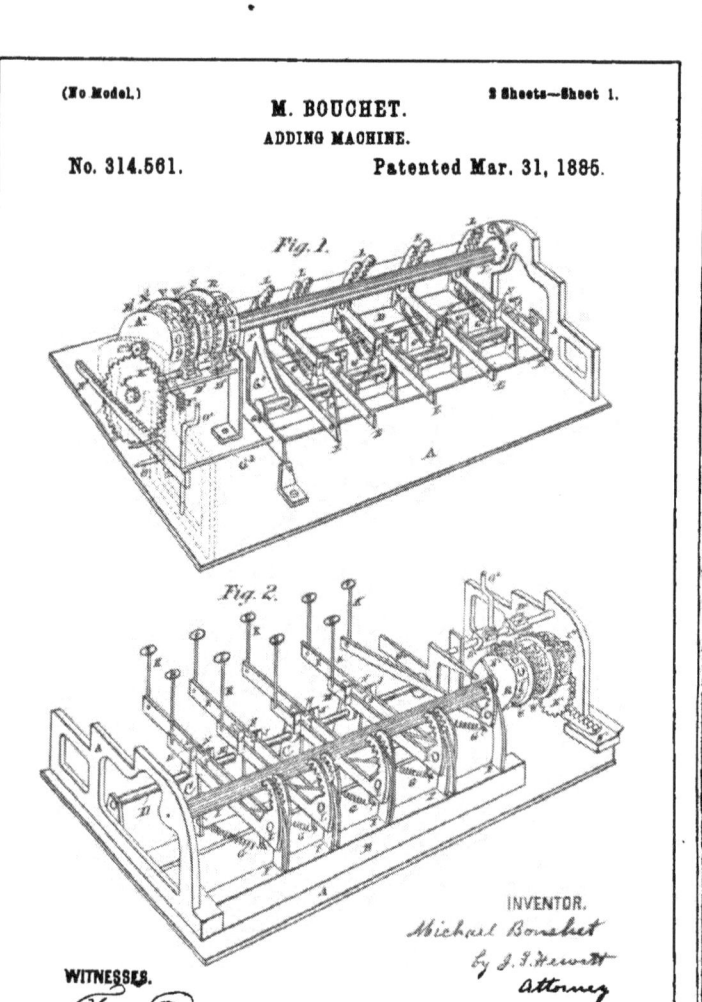

From Drawings of Bouchet Patent 314,561

gear-toothed rack and that the key stem is provided with a projecting arm ending in a downwardly projecting tooth or detent which may engage the rotor E, and stop it at the end of the downward key action. While the stopping of the rotor shows a control in the Robjohn machine which takes place under direct action from the keys to prevent overthrow of the units numeral wheel, it did not prevent the overflow of the higher or tens wheels, if a carry should take place. There was no provision for a control of the numeral wheels under the action received from the carry of the tens by the transfer mechanism.

The first attempt to control the carried wheel in a key-driven machine is found in a patent issued to Bouchet in 1882 (see illustration on opposite page); but it was a Geneva motion gearing which, as is generally known, may act to transmit power and then act to lock the wheel to which the power has been transmitted until it is again to be turned through the same source. Such a geared up and locked relation between the numeral wheels, of course, made the turning of the higher wheel (which had been so locked) by another set of key-mechanism an impossibility.

First control for a carried numeral wheel

BOUCHET MACHINE

The illustration of the Bouchet machine on the opposite page was reproduced from the drawings of the patent which is the nearest to the machine that was placed on the market. The numeral wheels, like most of the single-digit adders, are three in number, and consist of the prime actuated, or units wheel, and two overflow wheels to receive the carry of the tens. The units wheel has fixed to it a long 10-tooth pinion or rotor I, with which nine internal segmental gear racks L, are arranged to engage and turn the units wheel through their nine varying additive degrees of rotation.

Description of Bouchet machine

The segmental gear racks L, are normally out of mesh with the pinion I, and are fast to the key levers E, in such a manner that the first depression of a key causes its rack to rock forward and engage with the pinion I, and further depression moves the rack upward and rotates the pinion and units numeral wheel. It will be noted that this engaging and disengaging gear action is in principle like that of Robjohn.

The transfer devices for the carry of the tens, as already stated, belong to that class of mechanism commonly known as the "Geneva motion." It consists of a mutilated or one-tooth gear fast to the units wheel operating with a nine-tooth gear, marked D^1, loosely mounted on an axis parallel to the numeral wheel axis. Each revolution of the units wheel moves the nine-tooth gear three spaces, and in turn moves the next higher numeral wheel to which it is geared far enough to register one point or the carry. A circular notched disc, marked S, is fast to the units wheel, and the nine-tooth gear D^1, has part of two out of every three of its teeth mutilated or cut away to make a convex surface for the notched disc to rotate in.

With such construction the nine-tooth gear may not rotate or become displaced as long as the periphery of the disc continues to occupy any one of the three convex spaces of the nine-tooth gear. When, however, the notch of the disc is presented to the mutilated portion of the nine-tooth gear, the said gear is unlocked. This unlocking is coincident to the engagement of the single tooth of the numeral wheel-gear with the nine-tooth gear and the passing of the numeral wheel from 9 to 0, during which the nine-tooth gear will be moved three spaces, and will be again locked as the notch in the disc passes and the periphery fills the next convex space of the mutilated nine-tooth gear.

The Bouchet machine was manufactured and sold to some extent, but never became popular, as it lacked capacity. Machines of such limited capacity could not compete with ordinary accountants, much less with those who could mentally add from two to four columns at a clip. Aside from the capacity feature, there was another reason why these single-order machines were useless, except to those who could not add mentally. Multiple forms of calculation, that is, multiplication and division, call for a machine having a multiplicity of orders. The capacity of a single order would be but 9×9, which requires no machine at all—a seven-year-old child knows that. To multiply 58964×6824, however, is a different thing, and requires a multiple-order calculator.

Bouchet machine marketed

It is perhaps well at this time to point out the misuse of the term calculating where it is applied to machines having only a capacity for certain forms of calculating as compared with machines which perform in a practical way all forms of calculation, that is, addition, multiplication, subtraction and division. To apply the term "calculating machine" to a machine having anything less than a capacity for all these forms is erroneous.

Misuse of the term "Calculating Machine"

An adding machine may perform one of the forms of calculation, but to call it a calculating machine when it has no capacity for division, subtraction or multiplication, is an error; and yet we find the U. S. Patent Office records stuffed full of patents granted on machines thus erroneously named. The term calculating is the broad term covering all forms of calculation, and machines performing less should be designated according to their specific capacities.

It is true that adding is calculating, and under these circumstances, why then may not an adding machine be called a calculator? The answer is that it may be calculating to add; it may be calculating to either subtract, multiply or divide; but if a machine adds and is lacking in the means of performing the other forms of calculation, it is only part of a calculating machine and lacks the features that will give it title to being a full-fledged calculator.*

Considerable contention was raised by parties in a late patent suit as to what constituted the make-up of a calculating machine. One of the attorneys contended that construction was the only thing that would distinguish a calculating machine. But as machines are named by their functioning, the contention does not hold water. That is to say: A machine may be a calculating machine and yet its construction be such that it performs its functions of negative and positive calculation without reversal of its action.

Again, a machine may be a calculating machine and operate in one direction for positive calculation and the reverse for negative calculation. As long as the machine has been so arranged that all forms of calculation may be performed by it with-

* NOTE: The title of this book does not coincide with the above argument, but in view of the common use of the term "calculating" its application is better understood.

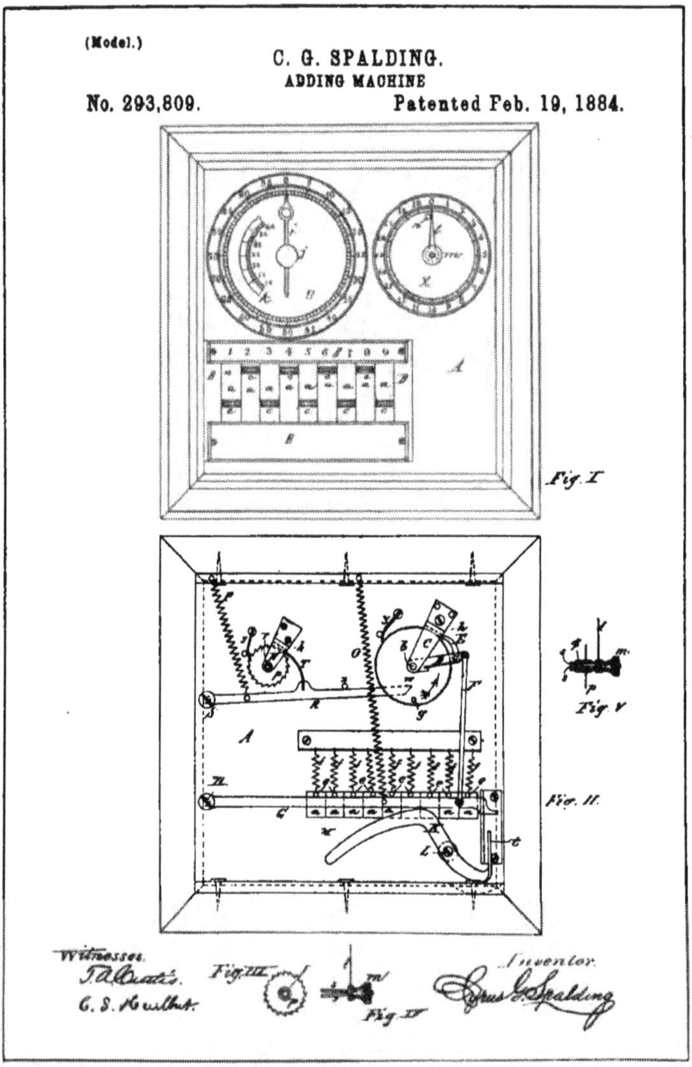

(Model.)

C. G. SPALDING.
ADDING MACHINE

No. 293,809.   Patented Feb. 19, 1884.

Drawings of Spalding Patent No. 293,809

out mental computation, and the machine has a reasonable capacity of at least eight orders, it should be entitled to be called a calculating machine.

THE SPALDING MACHINE

The next machine that has any bearing on the key-driven Art of which there is a record, is illustrated in a patent granted to C. G. Spalding in 1884 (see illustration on opposite page). The Spalding invention, like that of Bouchet, was provided with control for its primary actuation and control for its secondary or carrying actuation.

Referring to the Spalding machine reproduced from the drawings of his patent, the reader will note that in place of the units and tens numeral wheels, a clock hand has been supplied, co-operating with a dial graduated from 0 to 99, showing the figures 5, 10, 15, etc., to 95, for every five graduations.

Description of Spalding machine

Another similar hand or arrow and dial to register the hundreds is also provided, having a capacity to register nineteen hundred. Attached to the arrows, through a shaft connection at the back of the casing are ratchet wheels, having respectively the same number of teeth as the graduation of the dial to which each hand belongs.

Co-operating with the hundred-tooth ratchet of the units and tens register hand is a ratchet and lever motion device (see Fig. 2) to turn the arrow from one to nine points of the graduation of the dial. The ratchet and lever-motion device consists of the spring-pressed pawl E, mounted on the lever arm D, engaging the hundred-tooth ratchet, the link or push-rod F, the lever G, and its spring O. It will be noted that a downward action of the lever G, will, through the rod F, cause a like downward action of the lever D, causing the ratchet pawl E to be drawn over the ratchet teeth. Upon the release of the lever G, the spring O, will return it to its normal position and through the named connecting parts, ratchet forward the arrow.

The normal position of the pawl E is jammed into the tooth of the ratchet and against the bracket C, that forms the pivot support for the pivot shaft of the arrow. This jammed or locked combination serves to stop the momentum of the ratchet wheel at the end of the ratcheting action, and holds the wheel and its arrow normally locked until the lever G is again depressed.

The means for gauging the depression and additive degrees of action of the lever G is produced through the slides or keys marked a, having finger-pieces c, springs f, and pins e, bearing against the top of the lever G, combined with what may be called a compensating lever marked K.

The specification of the patent states that the depression of a key will depress the lever G and the free end will engage the bent end t, of the compensating lever K, and rock its envolute curved arm M, upward until it engages the pin e of the key, which will block further motion of the parts.

The effectiveness of the construction shown for the lever K is open to question.

The carry of the hundreds is accomplished by means of a one-step ratchet device represented by the parts lever R, pawl T, spring P, and operating pin g. When the hundred-tooth ratchet nears the end of its revolution, the pin g, made fast therein, engages the free end of the ratchet lever R, and depresses it; and as the hand attached to the hundred-tooth ratchet wheel passes from 99 to 0 the pin g passes off the end of the ratchet lever R, and the spring P retracts the lever ratcheting the twenty-tooth wheel and its arrow forward one point so that the arrow registers one point greater on the hundreds dial.

Prime actuation of a carried wheel impossible in the Spalding machine

Although the Spalding means of control under carrying differed from that of Bouchet in construction, its function was virtually the same in that it locked the carried or higher wheel in such a manner as to prevent the wheel from being operated by an ordinal set of key mechanism.

And the control under key action would prevent a carry being delivered to that order through the locked relation of the ratchet and pawl E.

The Key-Driven Calculator

WHILE these single digit adding machines have been used to illustrate how the control, which was lacking in the Hill invention, had been recognized by other inventors as a necessary requisite to the key-drive, it should not be construed that such carrying control as had been applied to their inventions was of a type that could be used in the Hill machine or in any multiple-order key-driven machine. It was thirty years after the first attempt to control a key-driven machine was made before an operative multiple-order key-driven machine, with a control that would prevent over-rotation, was finally invented.

Theory versus the concrete

Theoretically, it would seem that the only feature or element lacking in the Art prior to 1886, to produce a real key-driven calculator was means that would control the carrying and also leave the carried wheel free for key actuation. It was, however, quite a different problem. Theoretical functions may be patched together to make a theoretical machine; but that is only theory and not the concrete.

To take fragmental parts of such machines as were disclosed in the Art and patch them together into anything practical was impossible, even if one had been familiar with the Art and could devise mechanism to supply the new element. That is, leaving aside the broad or generic theoretical elements, which today, from knowledge gained by later inventions, serve the make-up of a key-driven calculator, there was still lacking any concrete example or specific design of a whole machine, as there was no such machine disclosed in the drawings of patents, or any known mechanism which, if arranged in multiples, would be operative as a practical machine even if mechanism to supply the new element were to be added.

All but one of the generic elements solved

In other words, while it is conceded from our present knowledge that all but one of the generic theoretical elements had been solved as disclosed in the various before-named machines, it required the application of these elements in a different way from anything before disclosed; which in itself required a different concrete form of the generic principles for the whole machine as well as a generic form of invention covering the new theoretical element.

It may be easy to analyze that which exists, but quite a different story to conceive that which did not exist. With reference to the Art, however, the production of the new element is a feature that may be credited without question. The concrete does not enter into it other than as proof that a new feature has been created.

While the discussion of the Art from a scientific standpoint brings together in after years what has been accomplished by different inventors, it is doubtful whether any of these early inventors had other knowledge than what may possibly have been obtained from seeing one of the foreign-made crank-driven machines. All inventors work with an idea obtained from some source, but on the whole few copy inventions of others. When an Art is fully established, however, and machines representing

Originality of inventions

the Art are to be found on the market and the principal features of such machines are portrayed in a later patent, it may rightly be called a copy. To assume, however, that a novice has taken the trouble to delve into the archives of the patent office and study the scattered theoretical elements of the Art and supply a new element to make a combination that is needed to produce a practical key-driven calculator, is not a probable assumption. But allowing such assumption were possible, it is evident that from anything that the Art disclosed prior to 1887 it was not possible to solve the concrete production of a key-driven calculator.

A conception which led to the final solution

In 1884, a young machinist, while running a planer, conceived an idea from watching its ratchet feed motion, which was indirectly responsible for the final solution of the multiple-order key-driven calculating machine. The motion, which was like that to be found on all planing machines, could be adjusted to ratchet one, two, three, four or more teeth for a fine or coarse feed.

While there is nothing in such a motion that would in any way solve the problem of the modern calculator, it was enough to excite the ambitions of the man who did finally solve it. It is stated that the young man, after months of thought, made a wooden model, which he finished early in 1885. This model is extant, and is illustrated on the opposite page.

The inventor was Dorr E. Felt, who is well known in the calculating-machine Art as the manufacturer of the "Comptometer," and in public life as a keen student of economic and scientific subjects. The wooden model, as will be noted, was crude, but it held the nucleus of the machine to come.

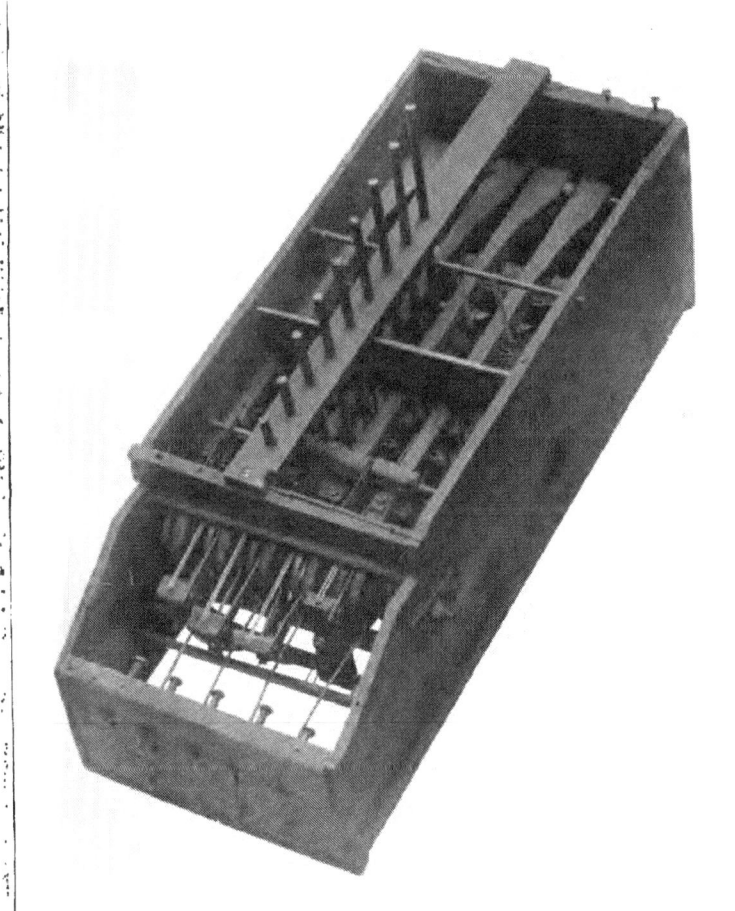

"Macaroni Box" Model

Mr. Felt has given some interesting facts regarding his experience in making the wooden model.

He says: "Watching the planer-feed set me to scheming on ideas for a machine to simplify the hard grind of the bookkeeper in his day's calculation of accounts.

Evolution of an invention

"I realized that for a machine to hold any value to an accountant, it must have greater capacity than the average expert accountant. Now I knew that many accountants could mentally add four columns of figures at a time, so I decided that I must beat that in designing my machine. Therefore, I worked on the principle of duplicate denominational orders that could be stretched to any capacity within reason. The plan I finally settled on is displayed in what is generally known as the "Macaroni Box" model. This crude model was made under rather adverse circumstances.

"The construction of such a complicated machine from metal, as I had schemed up, was not within my reach from a monetary standpoint, so I decided to put my ideas into wood.

"It was near Thanksgiving Day of 1884, and I decided to use the holiday in the construction of the wooden model. I went to the grocer's and selected a box which seemed to me to be about the right size for the casing. It was a macaroni box, so I have always called it the macaroni box model. For keys I procured some meat skewers from the butcher around the corner and some staples from a hardware store for the key guides and an assortment of elastic bands to be used for springs. When Thanksgiving day came I got up early and went to work with a few tools, principally a jack knife.

Trials of an inventor

Dorr E. Felt

"I soon discovered that there were some parts which would require better tools than I had at hand for the purpose, and when night came I found that the model I had expected to construct in a day was a long way from being complete or in working order. I finally had some of the parts made out of metal, and finished the model soon after New Year's day, 1885."

The first "Comptometer"

By further experimenting the scheme of the wooden model was improved upon, and Felt produced, in the fall of 1886, a finished practical machine made of metal. This machine is illustrated on the opposite page.

THE FELT CALCULATING MACHINE

Referring to the illustration of Felt's first metal machine, it will be noted that the machine has been partly dismantled. The model was robbed of some of its parts to be used as samples for the manufacture of a lot of machines that were made later. In view of the fact that this machine is the first operative multiple-order key-driven calculating machine made, it seems a shame that it had to be so dismantled; but the remaining orders are operative and serve well to demonstrate the claims held for it.

Felt patent 371,496

The mechanism of the machine is illustrated in the reproduction of the drawings of Felt's patent, 371,496, on page 58. The specification of this patent shows that it was applied for in March, 1887, and issued October 11, 1887.

From the outward appearance of the machine it has the same general scheme of formation as is disclosed in the wooden model.

The constructional scheme of the mechanism consists of a series of numeral wheels, marked A

The First "Comptometer"

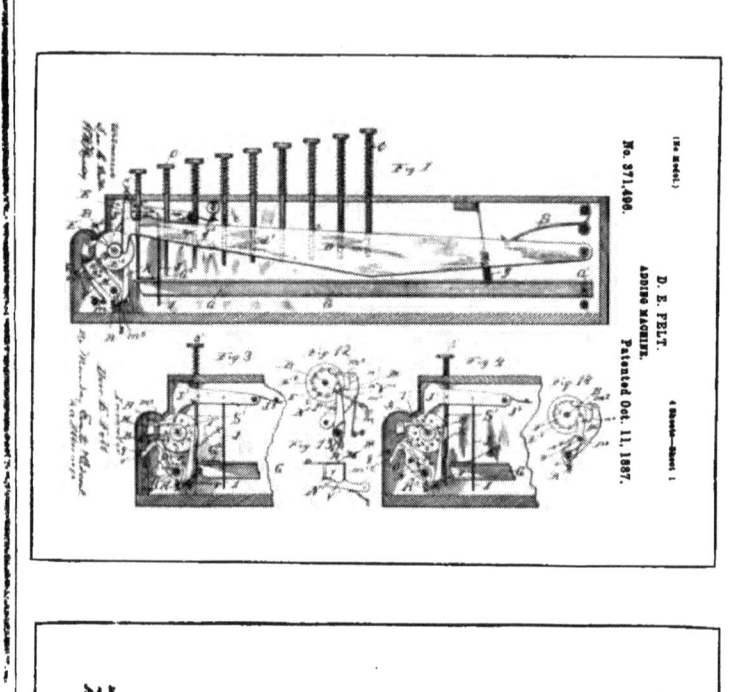

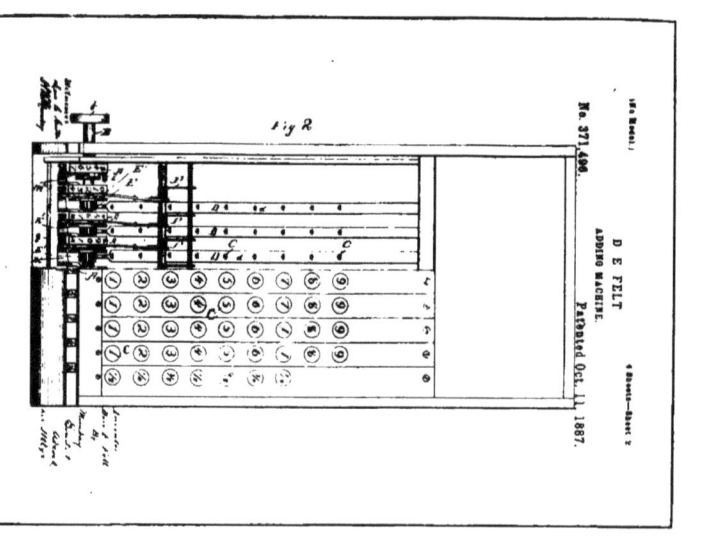

From Drawings of Felt Patent No. 371,496

in the patent drawings. Each wheel is provided with a ratchet wheel, and co-acting with the ratchet is a pawl mounted on a disc E^2, carried by the pinion E^1, which is rotatably mounted on the same axis as the numeral wheel. The arrangement of these parts is such that a rotating motion given any of the pinions E^1, in a clockwise direction, as shown in the drawings, would give a like action to their respective numeral wheels; but any motion of the pinions in an anti-clockwise direction would have no effect on the numeral wheels, owing to back-stop pawls K, and stop-pins T, provided to allow movement of the numeral wheels in but one direction.

Description of Felt calculator

Co-acting with each pinion E^1, is shown a long lever D, pivoted at the rear of the machine and provided with a segmental gear rack which meshes with the teeth of the pinion E^1. This lever comes under what is now generally termed a segment lever.

Each lever is provided with a spring S, which normally holds the front or rack end upward in the position shown in Fig. 1, and has co-acting with it a series of nine depressable keys which protrude through the casing and contact with the upper edge of the lever.

The arrangement of the keys with their segment levers provides that the depression of any key will depress the segment lever of that order, which in turn will rotate the pinion E^1 and its numeral wheel.

While this arrangement is such that each key of a series gives a different degree of leverage action to the segment lever, and in turn a degree of rotation to the numeral wheel of the same order in accordance with the numerical value of the key depressed, it may be conceived that the momentum set up by the quick stroke of a key would set the numeral wheel spinning perhaps two or three revolutions, or at any rate way beyond the point it should stop at to register correctly.

To preserve correct actuation of the mechanism and overcome its momentum, Felt provided a detent toothed lever for each numeral wheel, which will be found marked J^1 in the drawings. To this lever he linked another lever G, which extended below the keys, and arranged the length of the key stems so that when each key had revolved the numeral wheel the proper distance, the key will have engaged the lever G, and through the link connection will have caused the detent tooth of the lever J^1 to engage one of the pins T, of the numeral wheel, thus bringing the numeral wheel and the whole train of mechanism to a dead stop.

This combination was timed so that the (1) key would add one, the (2) key would add two, etc., up to nine for the (9) key. Thus the prime actuation of each wheel was made safe and positive.

Recapitulation of Art prior to Felt calculator

Before explaining the means by which the carry of the tens was effected in the Felt machine without interfering with multiple-order prime actuation, it will perhaps help the reader to recapitulate on what the Art already offered.

Going back to the Art, prior to Felt's invention, there are a few facts worth reconsidering that point to the broadly new contributions presented in the Felt invention, and combining these facts with a little theory may perhaps give a clearer understanding of what was put into practice.

In most lines of mechanical engineering in the past, the term "theory" connected with mechanical construction was a bugaboo. But the solution of the modern calculating machine was wholly dependent upon it.

Let us summarize on the Art, prior to Felt's invention. A calculating machine that would calculate, if we eliminate the key-driven feature, was old. The key-driven feature applied to adding mechanism was old as adapted to a single-order machine with a capacity for adding only a single column of digits.

Hill attempted to make a multiple order key-driven machine, but failed because he did not theorize on the necessities involved in the physical laws of mechanics.

Why Hill failed to produce an operative machine

Hill saw only the columnar arrangement of the ordinal division of the keyboard, and his thought did not pass beyond such relation of the keys for conveyance. There is no desire to belittle this feature, but it did not solve the problem that was set forth in the specification and claims of his patent; neither did it solve it for anyone else who wished to undertake the making of such a machine.

The introduction of keys as a driving feature in the calculating machine Art demanded design and construction suitable to control the new idiosyncrasies of force and motion injected into the Art by their use, of which the elements of inertia and momentum were the most troublesome.

Idiosyncrasies of force and motion increased by use of keys

Hill, in the design and construction of his machine, ignored these two elementary features of mechanics and paid the penalty by defeat. The tremendous speed transmitted to the parts of a key-driven machine, which has already been illustrated, required that lightness in construction which is absolutely necessary to reduce inertia to

Light construction a feature

a minimum, should be observed. The Hill machine design is absolutely lacking in such thought. The diameter of the numeral wheel and its heavy construction alone show this. Lightness of construction also enters into the control of momentum when the mechanism must suddenly be brought to a dead stop in its lightning-speed action. A heavily-constructed numeral wheel like that shown in the Hill patent would be as hard to check as it would to start, even if Hill had provided means for checking it.

Strength of design and construction, without the usual increase in weight to attain such end, but above all, the absolute control of momentum, were features that had to be worked out.

Robjohn partly recognized these features, but he limited the application of such reasoning to the prime actuation of a single order, and made nothing operable in a multiple key-driven machine.

Spalding and Bouchet recognized that the application of control was necessary for both prime actuation and carrying, but, like Robjohn, they devised nothing that would operate with a series of keys beyond a single order.

Operative features necessary

An operative principle for control under prime actuation was perhaps present in some of the single-order key-driven machines, but whatever existed was applied to machines with keys arranged in the bank form of construction, and, to be used with the keys in columnar formation, required at least a new constructive type of invention. But none of the means of control for carrying, prior to Felt's invention, held any feature that would solve the problem in a multiple-order machine.

While all the machines referred to have not been illustrated and described here, fair samples of the type that have any pertinence to the Art have been discussed, and those not illustrated would add nothing more than has been shown. A classification of the inventions referred to may be made as follows:

Parmelee and Stetner had no carrying mechanism; Hill, Robjohn, Borland and Hoffman, Swem, Lindholm and Smith had no control for the carry. Carroll, Bouchet and Spalding show a control for the carrying action, which in itself would defeat the use of a higher wheel for prime actuation, and which obviously would also defeat its use in a multiple-order key-driven machine.

One of the principal reasons why theory was necessary to solve the problem of the key-driven calculator existed in the impossibility of seeing what took place in the action of the mechanism under the lightning speed which it receives in operation. Almost any old device could be made to operate if moved slow enough to see and study its action; but the same mechanism that would operate under slow action would not operate correctly under the lightning-speed action they could receive from key depression. Only theoretical reasoning could be used to analyze the cause when key-driven mechanism failed to operate correctly.

Referring again to the drawings of the Felt patent, which illustrate the first embodiment of a multiple-order key-driven calculating machine, we find, what Felt calls in the claims and specifications, a carrying mechanism for a multiple-order key-driven calculating machine. This mechanism was, as set forth in the specification, a mechanism

Classification of the features contained in the early Art of key-driven machines

Carrying mechanism of Felt's calculator

for transferring the tens, which have been accumulated by one order, to a higher order, by adding one to the wheel of higher order for each accumulation of ten by the lower order wheel. This, in the Felt machine, as in most machines, was effected by the rotation of a numbered drum, called the numeral wheel, marked with the nine digits and cipher.

Transfer devices

The term "transfer device" for such mechanism was in common use, and as a term it fits certain parts of all classes of devices used for that purpose, whether for a crank-driven, key-driven, or any other type of multiple-order or single-order machine. But in the Felt invention we find it was not the simple device generally used for transferring the tens. It was, in fact, a combination of devices co-acting with each other which, in the specification of the patent, was termed the carrying mechanism.

Now, carrying mechanism may in a sense be termed a transfer device, as one of its functions is that of transferring power to carry the tens, but a mere transfer device may not be truthfully termed a carrying mechanism for a multiple-order key-driven machine unless it performs the functions that go to make up a correct carrying of the tens in that class of machine, and which we find laid down under the head of carrying mechanism in the Felt patents, where we find the first operative carrying mechanism ever invented for a multiple-order key-driven machine.

Carrying mechanism versus mere transfer devices

The functions demanded of such a piece of mechanism are as follows: First, the storing of power to perform the carry; second, the unlocking of the numeral wheel to be carried; third, the delivery of the power stored to perform such carry; fourth, the stopping and locking of the carried wheel when it has been moved to register such carry; and fifth, clearing the carrying-lock during prime actuation. A seemingly simple operation, but let those who have tried to construct such mechanism judge; they at least have some idea of it and they will no doubt bow their heads in acknowledgment of the difficulties involved in this accomplishment.

Mechanism for carrying the tens in single digit adders was one thing, and such as was used could well bè called a transfer device; but mechanism for carrying the tens in a real key-driven calculating machine was another thing, and a feature not solved until Felt solved it, and justly called such combination of devices a "carrying mechanism."

In the Felt machine, the carrying mechanism consisted of a lever and ratchet pawl action, constructed of the parts M, m², operated by a spring m, the pawl acting upon the numeral wheel pins T, to ratchet the wheel forward under the spring power. The power in the spring was developed from the rotation of the lower wheel, which through the means of an envolute cam* attached to left side of each wheel, operated the carrying lever in the opposite direction to that in which it was operated by the spring. As the carrying lever passed the highest point of the cam spiral and dropped off, the stored power in the spring retracted the lever M, and the pawl m², acting on the higher order wheel pins T, and moved it one-tenth of a revolution.

*Note: As all the drawings of the Felt patent are not reproduced here, the cam is not shown.

Details of Felt carrying mechanism

This part of the mechanism was in principle an old and commonly-used device for a one-step ratchet motion used in the carry of the tens. It served as a means of storing and transferring power from the lower wheel to actuate the higher wheel in a carrying operation, but a wholly unqualified action without control.

In the Felt machine a spring-actuated lever N, mounted on the same axis with the carrying lever, and provided with a detent stop-hook at its upper end, served to engage the numeral wheel at the end of its carried action, and normally hold it locked.

An arm or pin P, fixed in and extending from the left side of the carrying lever and through a hole in the detent lever, acted to withdraw the detent lever from its locking engagement with the numeral wheel as the carrying lever reached the extreme point of retraction; thus the wheel to be carried was unlocked.

Pivoted to the side of the detent lever is a catch O. This catch or latch is so arranged as to hook on to a cross-rod q, especially constructed to coact with the catch and hold the detent-lever against immediate relocking of the numeral wheel as the carrying lever and pawl act in a carrying motion. The latch has a tail or arm p, which coacts with the pin P on the carrying lever in such a way as to release the latch as the carrying lever finishes its carrying function.

Thus the detent lever N is again free to engage one of the control or stop-pins T to stop and lock the carried numeral wheel when the carrying lever and pawl, through the action of the spring stored in the carrying, has moved the wheel the proper distance.

Chicago, Feb. 28th 1887

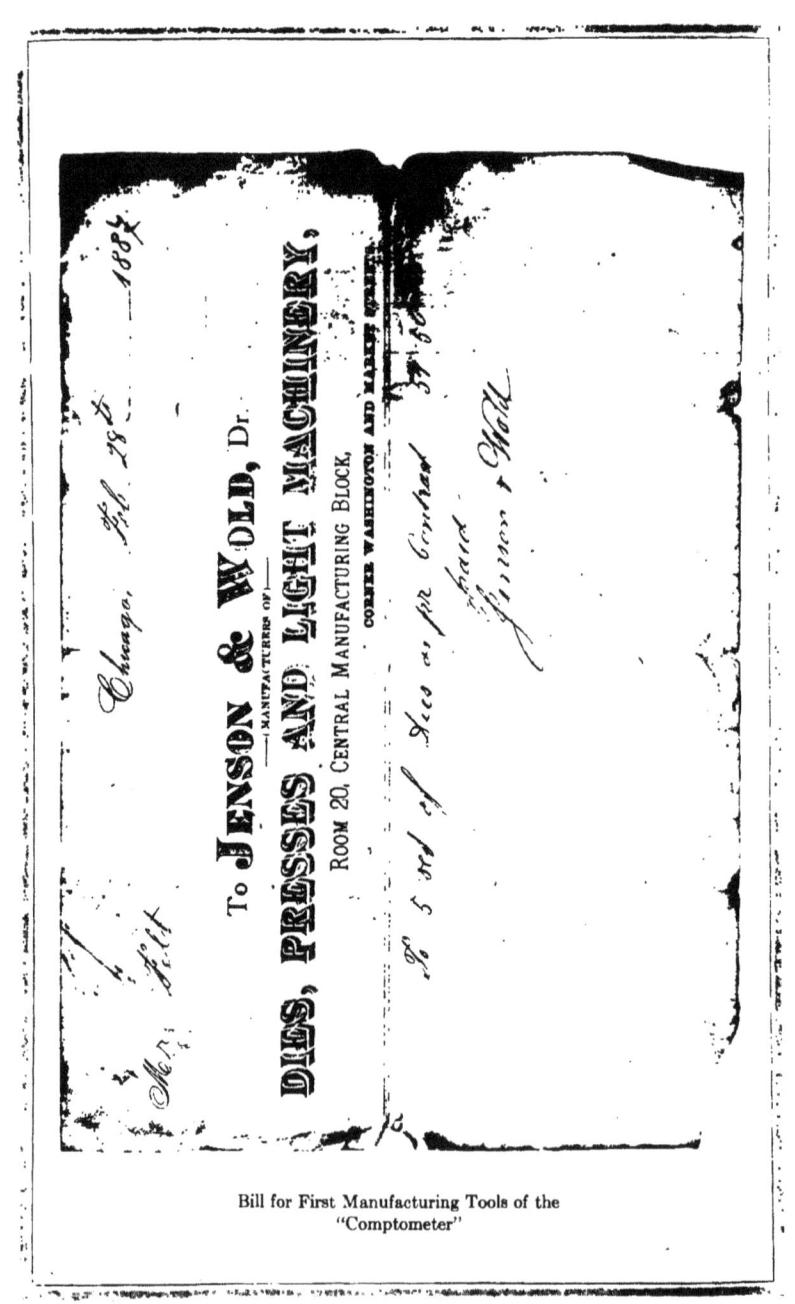

Mr. Felt

To **JENSON & WOLD,** Dr.
— MANUFACTURERS OF —
DIES, PRESSES AND LIGHT MACHINERY,
ROOM 20, CENTRAL MANUFACTURING BLOCK,
CORNER WASHINGTON AND HALSTED STS.

To 5 std of dies as per Contract $39.50
Paid
Jenson & Wold

Bill for First Manufacturing Tools of the
"Comptometer"

A lot of functions to take place in 1/165 of a second, but it worked. The timing of the stop and locking detents, of course, was one of the finest features.

The normal engagement of the carrying detent, it may be understood, would prevent the movement of the wheel by key action or prime actuation, but the patent shows how Felt overcame this.

The carrying stop and locking detent lever N is provided with a cam-arm or pin N, which was arranged to co-act with the cam disc E (see Fig. 1), fast to the prime actuating pinion E. The cam surface was short and performed its function during a short lost motion arranged to take place before the ratchet pawl would pick up and move the numeral wheel under key actuation.

The camming action was outward and away from the center, and thus released the carrying stop from its locking position with the numeral wheel, and continued rotation of the pinion and cam disc would hold the lock out of action until the parts had returned to normal.

With the return action of the keys, segment lever, pinion and cam disc, through the action of a spring attached to the segment lever, the carrying stop detent will again engage and lock the numeral wheel.

Felt really started to manufacture his calculating machine in the fall of 1886, after perfecting his invention. Having only a very limited amount of money with which to produce machines, young Felt, then but 24 years of age, was obliged to make the machines himself, but with the aid of some dies which he had made for some of the principal parts (see reproduction of bill for dies on opposite page), he was able to produce eight finished

Manufacture of the Felt calculator

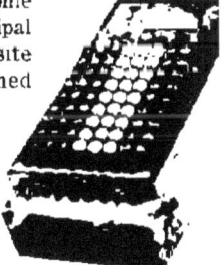

Early Comptometer

machines before September, 1887. Two of these machines were immediately put into service, for the training of operators, as soon as they were finished.

Trade name of Felt calculator

Of the first trained operators to operate these machines, which were given the trademark name "Comptometer," one was Geo. D. Mackay, and another was Geo. W. Martin. After three or four months' practice Mr. Martin demonstrated one of these machines to such firms as Sprague, Warner & Co., Pitkin & Brooks, The Chicago Daily News, and the Chicago, Burlington & Quincy R. R. Co., and finally took employment with the Equitable Gas Light & Fuel Co. of Chicago (see letter on opposite page) as operator of the "Comptometer." The Gas Co. has since been merged with several other companies into the Peoples Gas Light & Coke Co. of Chicago.

A very high testimonial of the qualities of the Felt invention was given by Mr. Martin in 1888, a year after he entered the employment of the Gas Co., and is reproduced on page 72.

Another fine testimonial was given by Geo. A. Yulle, Secy. & Treas. of the Chicago Gas Light & Coke Co., in September, 1888 (see page 74). Mr. Mackay, the other operator, secured employment with Albert Dickinson & Co., Seed Merchants, as operator of the "Comptometer." Mr. Mackay was interviewed a few months ago, and was at that time, after thirty years, still with the same firm, and a strong advocate of the "Comptometer."

Felt calculator Exhibit at National Museum

In September, 1887, Felt took one of the first eight machines to Washington and exhibited it to Gen. W. S. Rosecrans, then Registrar of the Treasury, and left the machine in the office of Dr.

Chicago, Nov 6, 1887

Mr. Ows Delt,

Dear Sir:—

Your favor of the 2nd inst. was delivered yesterday at 11 o'clock A. M. and in accordance with your request I have called on as many business men as I will have time to call, owing to the fact that the Ins Co has written for me to come to work next Monday morning. The names and addresses are as follows: Sprague Warner & Co, Michigan Ave and Randolph; Pitkin & Brooks, Lake and State Sts; Melville E. Stone, Editor of Daily News, and the Freight Auditor of C. B. & Q. R. Ry. These Gentlemen are very much pleased with the machine, and say they will give it a trial as soon as you put it on the market.

I do not think Mr. Hartwell will be ready before two weeks.

Very Truly Yours,

G. W. Martin

Letter from Geo. W. Martin

Copy

The Equitable Gas Light & Fuel Company.
Chicago Nov 19 1888.

To whom it may concern:

This is to certify that I have used the Felt and Tarrant Comptometer during the past Thirteen Months, and can heartily recommend it for accuracy, rapidity, durability, and labor saving features.

It occupies but little space, weighs only a trifle, is very easily operated, never gets out of order, and in short, is "a thing of beauty" in any business house.

It will prove an invaluable adjunct to the counting room in every calculation of insurance, interest, brokerage, precentage, commissions etc. etc.

By its use I have attained my present position, and do not feel the least hesitancy in pronouncing it one of the unequalled aids of the Nineteenth Century.

F. H. Martin
Cashier.

Testimonial

Chicago Sept 22. 1888

Mr. D. E. Felt.
52 & 56 Illinois St.
(Chicago)

Dear Sir:—
We have had in our Office, for nearly a year now, one of your "Comptometers" & have given it a fair trial. It certainly possesses great merit. There is no doubt but what a party with a few months' practice could "doubly" "Discount" the most expert figurer. I think in this age of new & useful invention, you are in the first part of the list.

Yours Resp.
Geo. A. Yuille
Sec Treas Chicago Gas Lt Coke Co.

Testimonial

[illegible] should be addressed to the Register of the Treasury.

Treasury Department.

REGISTER'S OFFICE.

Washington, D.C., Oct. 31st., 1887. 188

Hall Type Writer Co.,
Salem, Mass.

Gentlemen—

The letter of your Mr. Dalton, inquiring as to my views regarding the qualities of your Mr. Felt's adding machine and the demand for such an instrument, is to hand.

All I can say to you is simply that I am favorably impressed with its practical working qualities, and willing to recommend the purchase of three or four such for the use of this office. Beyond this, everything is conjectural, except that its [illegible] is evidently a condition sine qua non to its being [illegible].

Very truly yours,

W. S. Rosecrans
Register.

U.S. Treasury Department
Washington, D.C. Nov. 4, 1887.

Mr. C. C. Dalton.
Hall Type Writer Co.
Salem, Mass.

Dear Sir:

Your communication to the Treasurer of the United States, enquiring relative to the working of the adding machine of Mr. D. E. Felt of Chicago has been referred to me for reply.

In response I will say that I have had in my possession for a few weeks, one of the machines referred to, and have had it in daily use, and am much pleased with its operations.

I shall be unable to give you an opinion in regard to the demand for the machines, as it will depend on its price, and durability.

Respectfully yours,

E. B. Elliott
Government Actuary.

Letters from Elliott and Rosecrans

E. B. Elliott, Actuary of the Treasury, where it was put into constant use. Proof of the date of this use of Felt's invention in the Treasury is set forth in the reproduction of two letters (see opposite page), one was written by Mr. Elliott and another by Gen. W. S. Rosecrans, in answer to an inquiry of the Hall Typewriter Co. of Salem, Mass. Another of the first eight machines was placed with Dr. Daniel Draper, of the N. Y. State Weather Bureau, New York City.

Felt finally closed a deal with Mr. Robert Tarrant of Chicago, whereby a partnership contract was signed November 28, 1887. The partnership was incorporated January 25, 1889, under the name of the Felt & Tarrant Mfg. Co., who are still manufacturing and selling "Comptometers" under that name.

Laying aside all the evidence set forth in the foregoing history of key-driven machines and their idiosyncrasies, significant proof of Felt's claim as the first inventor of the modern calculating machine is justified by the fact that no other multiple-order key-driven calculating machine was placed on the market prior to 1902.

Significant proof of Felt's claim of priority

Lest we lose sight of a most important feature in dealing with the Art of the Modern Calculator, we should call to mind the fact that as Felt was the originator of this type of machine, he was also the originator of the scheme of operation in its performance of the many and varied short cuts in arithmetical calculation.

The performance of calculation on machines of the older Art differed so entirely from the new that any scheme of operation that may have been devised for their use would lend nothing to the

Rules for operation an important factor of modern calculator

derivation of the new process for operating the key-driven machine of the new Art.

A superficial examination of one of the instruction books of the "Comptometer" will convince most any one that it is not only the mechanism of the machine that made the modern calculator so valuable to the business world, but also the schemes laid down for its use. The instructions for figuring Multiplication, Subtraction, Division, Square Root, Cube Root, Interest, Exchange, Discount, English Currency, etc., involved hard study to devise such simple methods and rules.

The instruction books written by Felt for the "Comptometer, the Modern Calculator," reflect the genius disclosed in the invention of the machine itself.

From Drawings of Barbour Patent No. 133,188

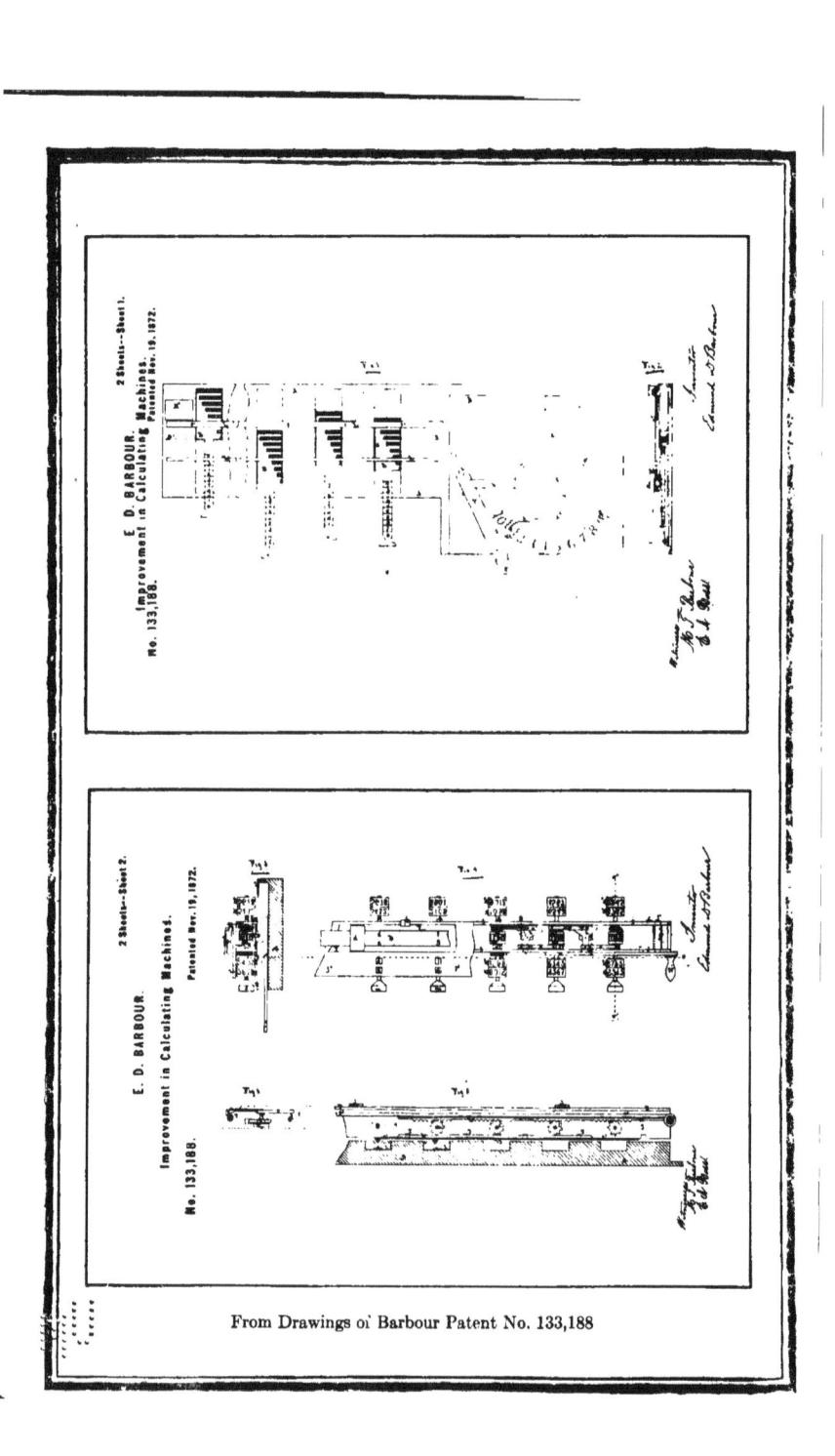

Early Efforts in the Recording Machine Art

THE Art of recording the addition of columns of figures is old in principle, but not in practice. Many attempts to make a machine that would record legibly under all conditions failed. These attempts have been pointed out from time to time as the first invention of the recording-adding machine, especially by those desirous of claiming the laurels.

The first attempt at arithmetical recording for which a patent was issued, was made by E. D. Barbour in 1872 (see illustration on opposite page).

First attempt to record arithmetical computation

E. D. Barbour has also the honor of being the first inventor to apply Napier's principle to mechanism intended to automatically register the result of multiplying a number having several ordinal places by a single digit without mentally adding together the overlapping figures resulting from direct multiplication. He patented this machine in 1872 just prior to the issue of his arithmetical recorder patent. (See page 181.)

The Barbour Machine

The printing device disclosed in connection with the Barbour machine for recording calculations was of the most simple nature, allowing only for the printing of totals and sub-totals.

Its manipulation consisted of placing a piece of paper under a hinged platen and depressing the platen by hand in the same manner that a time stamp is used. The ink had to be daubed on the type by a hand operation to make legible the impressions of the type.

Description of Barbour machine

The patent drawings of the Barbour machine are so fragmentary that it is almost impossible to draw any conclusion as to its functions without reading the specifications.

Fig. 1 represents the base of the machine, while Fig. 4 shows a carriage which, when in place, is superimposed above the base as illustrated in Figs. 3 and 5.

The operation of the machine is performed by first pulling out the slides B (shown in Fig. 1), which set the digital degrees of actuation of each order; and, second, by operating the hand-lever K, from its normal position at 0 to 1, if it is desired to add, or to any of the other numbers in accordance to the value of the multiplier if multiplication is desired.

The movement of the handle K, from one figure to the other, gives a reciprocation to the carriage, so that for each figure a reciprocation will take place.

Each of the slides B, has a series of nine gear racks; each rack has a number of teeth ranging progressively from 1 tooth for the first gear rack to 9 teeth for the last rack, thus the pulling out of the slides B will present one of the gear racks in line to act upon the accumulator mechanism of the carriage as the carriage is moved back and forth over it.

The accumulator mechanism consists of the register wheels M^1 and M^2 and the type wheels M^3

and M⁴ mounted on a common arbor and a carry transfer device between the wheels of each order.

Operating between the accumulator wheels and the racks of plate B are a pair of gears, one in the form of a lantern wheel loosely mounted on the accumulator wheel shaft but connected thereto by a ratchet wheel and pawl connection; the other, a small pinion meshing with the lantern wheel on a separate axis, protrudes below the carriage into the path of the racks.

Thus as the carriage is moved by the reciprocating device connected with the hand-lever K, the pinions of the accumulator will engage whatever racks have been set and the numeral wheels and type wheels will be operated to give the result.

The numeral and type wheels have two sets of figures, one of which is used for addition and multiplication, while the other set runs in the opposite direction for negative computation or subtraction and division.

A plate arranged with sight apertures covers the numeral or register wheels, while the type wheels are left uncovered to allow a hinged platen F, mounted on the top of the carriage (see Fig. 3), to be swung over on top of them and depressed.

Attached to the platen F, are a series of spring clips d, under which strips of paper may be slipped (as shown by D, in Fig. 4), and which serves to hold the paper while an impression is taken.

Thus the Barbour invention stands in the Art as something to show that as early as 1872 an effort was made to provide means to preserve a record of calculations by printing the totals of such calculations. *Barbour machine not practical*

THE BALDWIN MACHINE

The next effort in this class of machines is illustrated in a patent issued to Frank S. Baldwin in 1875 (see illustration on opposite page). The Baldwin machine is also of moment as having the scheme found in the machines known as the Brunsviga, made under the Odhner patents—a foreign invention, later than that of Baldwin, used extensively abroad and to a limited extent in this country.

The contribution of Baldwin to the Art of recording-calculating devices seems to be only the roll paper in ribbon form and the application of the ink ribbon. The method used by Barbour for type impression was adapted and used by Baldwin; that is, the hinged platen and its operation by hand.

Of the illustrations shown of the Baldwin machine, one is reproduced from the drawings of the patent while the other is a photo reproduction of the actual machine which was placed on the market, but, as may be noted, minus the printing or recording device shown in the patent drawings.

Description of Baldwin machine

Referring to the photo reproduction, the upper row of figures showing through the sight apertures in the casing are those of the numeral wheels which accumulate the totals, and which in the patent drawings would represent the type of the accumulator wheels for printing the totals of addition and multiplication or the remainders of subtraction and division.

The figures showing below serve to register multiples of addition and subtraction which would read as the multiplier in multiplications or the quotient in division. These wheels are the type

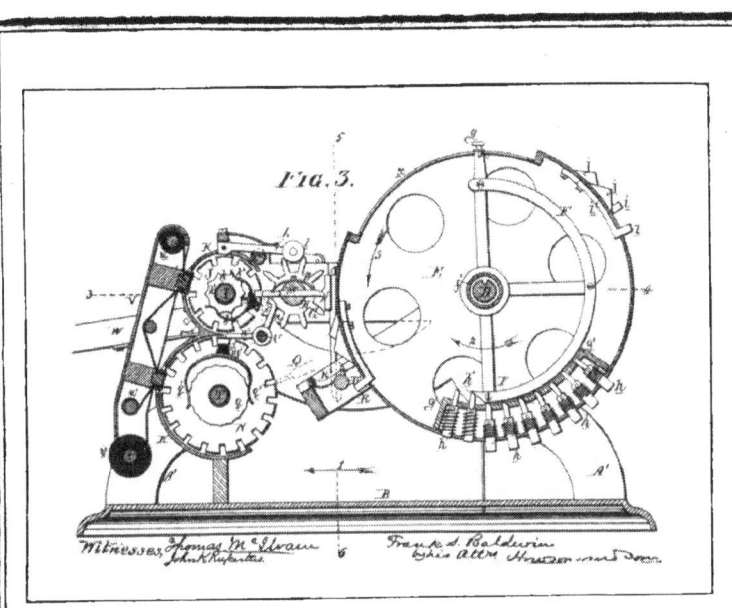

From Drawings of Baldwin Patent No. 159,244

Baldwin Machine

wheels N, in the patent drawings, which serve the purpose of recording the named functions of calculation.

The means by which the type wheels of the upper row are turned through the varying degrees of rotation they receive to register the results of calculation, consists of a crank-driven, revolvable drum, marked E, which is provided with several denominational series of projectable gear teeth h, which may be made to protrude through the drum by operation of the digital setting-knobs g, situated on the outside of the drum.

These knobs, as shown in the patent drawings, are fast to radial arms, each of which serves as one of three spokes of a half-wheel device, operating inside the drum and pivoted on the inner hub of the drum.

These half wheels marked F, in the drawings, by means of their cam faces h^1, serve to force the gear teeth out through the face of the drum, or let them recede under the action of their springs as the knobs g, are operated forward and back in the slots x, of the drum provided for the purpose.

As will be noted from the photographic reproduction of the machine, these slots are notched to allow the arms extending through them to be locked in nine different radial positions, and that each of these positions are marked progressively from 0 to 9.

This arrangement allows the operator to set up numbers in the different orders by springing the setting-knobs g to the left and pulling them forward to the number desired, where it will become locked in the notch when released. This action will have forced out as many gear teeth in each order as have been set up by the knobs g in their respective orders.

The lateral positions of the projectable gear-teeth correspond to the spacing of the type-wheels, and an intermediate gear G, meshing with each type, or register wheel, is loosely mounted on the shaft H, interposed between the said wheels and the actuating drum E, so that when the drum is revolved by the crank provided for that purpose, the gear-teeth protruding from the drum will engage the intermediate gears G, and turn them and their type or register wheels as many of their ten points of rotation as have been set up in their respective orders of the setting devices of the drum.

Revolving the drum in one direction adds, while revolving it in the opposite direction subtracts, and repeated revolutions in either direction give respectively the multiple forms of addition or subtraction which result in either multiplication or division, as the case may be.

The actuating drum E, is provided with means by which it may be shifted to the left to furnish means for multiplying by more than one factor and to simplify the process of division.

The means for the carry of the tens consist of a series of teeth i, formed by the bent end of a pivoted spring-pressed lever arm which is pivoted to the inside of the actuating drum with the tooth protruding through a slot in the drum, so arranged as to allow motion of the tooth in a direction parallel to the drum axis.

Normally these teeth are held in a position to escape engagement with the intermediate gears G, but provision is made for camming the teeth i,

From Drawings of Pottin Patent No. 312,014

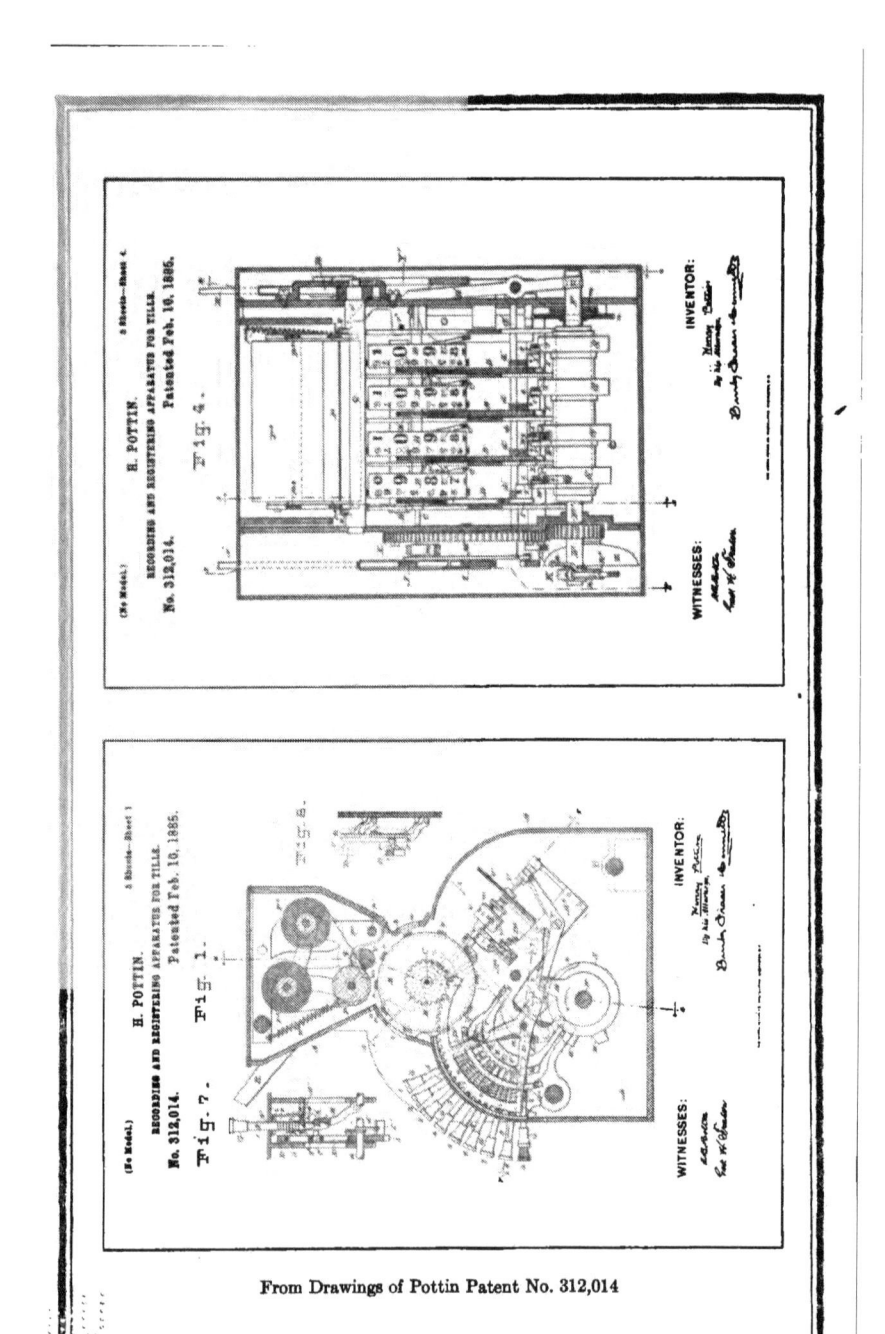

to the left into the path of an intermediate gear of one order as the type or register wheel of the lower order passes from 9 to 0.

The parts which perform this function are the cam m, located on the left side of each wheel, the plunger M, which operates in the fixed shaft H, and which has a T-shaped head that, when projected into the path of the carrying teeth i, serve to cam them sidewise and bring about the engagement referred to, which results in the higher type or numeral wheel being stepped forward one space.

The cam-lugs j on the drum serve to engage and push back the T heads of the cam plungers M, after they have brought about the one-step movement of the higher wheel.

The printing device consists of a hand-manipulated frame pivoted to the main frame of the machine by the shaft t. The paper is supplied from a roll about the shaft t, and an ink-ribbon is fed back and forth from the rolls u and u¹ over bars of the printing-frame which protrude through slots in the casing and act as platens for the impression of the paper and ink-ribbon against the type. *Baldwin's printing mechanism*

It is presumed that the paper was torn off after a record was printed in the same manner as in the more modern machines.

THE POTTIN MACHINE

Eight years after the Baldwin patent was issued, a Frenchman named Henry Pottin, residing in Paris, France, invented a machine for recording cash transactions, which he patented in England in 1883 and in the United States in 1886 (see illustration on opposite page).

The form and design of the machine, as will be noted, correspond quite favorably with the scheme of the present-day cash register, although it lacks the later refinement that has made the cash register acceptable from a visible point of view.

First key-set crank-operated machine and first attempt to record the items in addition

The Pottin invention is named here as the first in which two of the prime principles of the recording-adders of today are disclosed; one is the depressable key-set feature and the other is the recording of the numerical items. The Pottin machine was the first known depressable key-set crank-operated machine made to add columns of figures and the first machine in which an attempt was made to print the numerical items as they were added.

Turning to the illustration of the U. S. patent drawings of the Pottin machine, the reader will note that there are four large wheels shown, marked B. These wheels are what may be called the type-wheels, although they also serve as indicator wheels for registering cash sales. The type figures are formed by a series of needles fixed in the face of the wheels.

The means employed for presenting the proper type figure for printing and likewise the indicator figures to indicate the amount set up in each denominational order was as follows:

Referring to Fig. 1, it will be noted that to each type-wheel is geared a spring-actuated segmental rack marked D, which, as shown in the drawing, is in contact with a pin marked i, which protrudes from the side of the depressed number (9) key.

The normal position of the rack D, is indicated in dotted lines showing the next higher sector which has not been displaced by key depression.

Each key, as will be noted from Fig. 7, is provided with one of the pins i, which is normally out of the path of the lug j, as the racks D, drop forward; but when any key is depressed the pin is presented in the path of the lug j, and stops further forward action of the rack.

Description of Pottin machine

It will be noted that the arrangement of the keys is such as will allow progressively varying degrees of action to the segmental racks D. This variation, combined with the geared relation of the type-wheels and racks is equivalent to a tenth of a rotation of the type-wheel for each successive key in the order of their arrangement from 1 to 9.

The means provided for holding the segmental racks D, at normal, also serves to hold a key of the same order depressed, and consists of a pivoted spring-pressed latch-frame marked E (see Figs. 7 and 8).

With such a combination, the depression of keys in the several orders will unlatch the segmental racks, and the racks, through the tension of their actuating springs, will turn the wheels and present a type corresponding to the numerical value of each key depressed.

A hand lever, marked R, located on left side of the machine provides power for printing the items. Another hand lever, marked J, serves to restore the segmental racks, type-wheels and the keys to normal, and through the co-operation of the lever R, adds the items to the totalizer numeral wheels, which are shown in Fig. 1 as the numbered wheels marked v.

The paper is supplied from a roll mounted on a hinged platen frame P^1, supported in its normal position by a spring P^3. The paper passes under the roller P, which acts as a platen for the impression of the type. A shaft Q, passing under the frame P^1, is fast and rigidly connected on the left-hand side of the machine with the hand lever R, and acts as a pivot for the said lever and by means of lateral projections q, serves when the lever R is operated to engage the frame P^1, and depresses it until the needle types have pricked the numerical items through the paper.

A slit in the casing provided means for printing the item on a separate piece of paper or bill.

Although there is no means shown by which the paper is fed after an item is printed, it is claimed in the specification that the well-known means for such feeding may be employed. The actuating lever J referred to, is connected by a ratchet and geared action with the shaft F*, so that a revolution is given the said shaft each time the lever is operated.

To the shaft F, (see Fig. 1) is attached a series of arms H, one for each order, which, as the shaft revolves in the direction of the arrow, engages a lug marked I, on the segmental racks D, thus rocking the segments back to normal, turning the typewheels with them.

The return of the segment racks D, cause the back of the latch tooth f^1, (see Fig. 8) to engage the latch tooth f, of the latch bar E, camming it out of engagement with the keys so that any key that has been set will return by means of its own spring.

*Note: All the drawings of the Pottin patent are not shown here.

From Drawings of Burroughs Patent No. 388,118

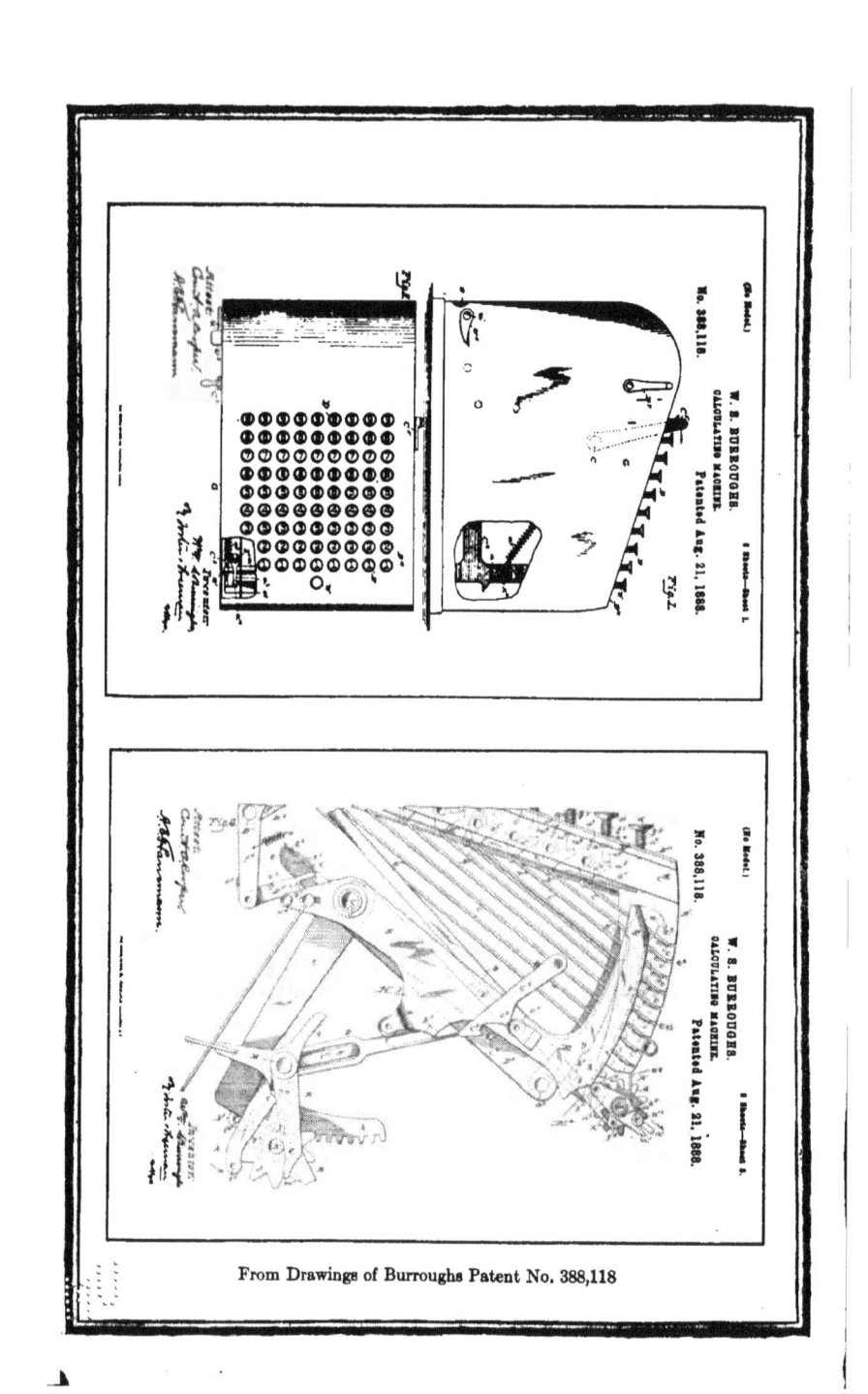

The total or accumulator numeral wheels are connectable with the type or indicating wheels B, by an engaging and disengaging gear motion set up by the combined action of the hand levers R and J, which first cause such gear engagement, and then, through the return of the type wheels to zero, turn the accumulator wheels, thus transferring the amount of the item set upon the type wheels to the accumulator wheels.

The specification claims the machine is intended for use by cashiers, bank-tellers, and others, to record receipts or disbursements.

It is also claimed in the specification that instead of the needle type ordinary type may be used in combination with an inking ribbon if so desired.

Early efforts of Wm. S. Burroughs

One of the next attempts to produce a recording-adder was made by Wm. S. Burroughs, whose name sixteen years later was used to rename the American Arithmometer Co., now known as the Burroughs Adding Machine Co.

The first patent issued to Burroughs, No. 388116, under date of August 21, 1888, like the machine of Barbour and Baldwin, was designed to record only the final result of calculation.

On the same date, but of later application, another patent, No. 388118, was issued to Burroughs which claimed to combine the recording of the numerical items and the recording of the totals in one machine. Some of the drawings of this patent have been reproduced. (See opposite page.)

MACHINE OF EARLY BURROUGHS PATENT

Referring to the drawings of the Burroughs patent, it will be noted, that in outward form, the machine is similar to the Burroughs machine

Wm. S. Burroughs

of today. To give a detailed description of the construction of the machine of this Burroughs patent would make tedious reading and take unnecessary space.

General scheme of Burroughs' first inventions

The principle involved in the mechanism for recording the items is very similar to that of the Pottin invention; the setting of the type wheels being effected as in the Pottin machine by means of segment gears which the depression of the keys serves to unlatch, and acts to gauge the additive degree of their movement.

Burroughs used the inking form of type proposed as an alternative by Pottin in his patent specification instead of the needles shown in the Pottin drawings.

In the Burroughs patent, as in the Pottin, it will be noted that there are two sets of wheels bearing figures, one set of which, marked J, situated at the rear, are the type-wheels, and the other set, marked A, at the front of the machine, are for the accumulation of the totals.

For each denominational order of the type and total wheels, there is provided an actuating segmental gear, consisting of a two-armed segmental lever pivoted to the shaft C, and having the gear teeth of its rear arm constantly in mesh with the pinion gear of the type-wheel J, and the gear teeth of the forward arm normally presented to, but out of mesh with the pinion gear of its total wheel A.

Each of these denominational actuators or segment gears is provided with a stop projection X^2, at the top end of its forward gear-rack, which serves as a means for interrupting the downward movement of that end of the segment lever, and thus controls its movement as a denominational actuator.

It will be noted that instead of the key-stems acting directly as a stop for the denominational actuators, as in the Pottin invention, Burroughs used a bell crank type of key lever and the stop-wire C^1 as an intermediate means, and in this manner produced a flat keyboard more practical for key manipulation.

The stop-wires C^1, as will be noted, are arranged to slide in slots of the framework, and while normally not presented in the path of the stop-projection X^2, of the denominational actuators, it may be observed that by the depression of the proper key any one of them may be drawn rearward and into the path of the stop projection X^2, of its related actuator, and thus serve as a means to intercept the downward action of the actuator.

Brief description of machine of early Burroughs patents

The denominational actuators in the Burroughs machine were not provided with spring tension that would cause them to act as soon as unlatched by depression of the keys as has been described in relation to the Pottin invention.

While the keys in the Burroughs machine, as in the Pottin invention, served also to unlatch the denominational actuators in their respective orders, no movement of the said actuators or type-wheels took place until a secondary action was performed.

The secondary action, or the operation of the hand lever, marked C^5, attached to the shaft C, on its initial or forward stroke dragged the denominational actuators down by means of friction and thus set the type-wheels, and by means claimed in the specification, brought about the type impression to print the result of the key-setting or the item so set.

The backward or rear stroke of the hand lever caused the accumulator or total numeral wheels to be engaged and the item to be added to them.

From this single lever action it will be noted that there is an improvement shown over and above the Pottin invention in the fact that but one lever motion is required; Pottin having provided two levers so that in the event of error the operation of one lever would reset the machine without performing any addition or printing.

In the Burroughs invention, the motion of denominational actuators and their type-wheels not being effected through depression of keys, as in the Pottin machine, allowed any error in the setting up of an item to be corrected by the resetting of the keys and relatching of the gears, which it is claimed was provided for by operation of the lever marked B^7 (Fig. 1 of the drawings).

As a means of supplying power to his denominational actuators, Burroughs provided what may be called a universal actuator common to all orders, composed of a rock frame (arms D^2, loose on each end of actuating shaft C, and having their outward ends rigidly connected by the bar a^9) and the arms E, fixed to each end of the shaft C.

Projecting from the inside of each of the arms E, are two lugs, b^1 and b^3, which contact with the arms D^2 of the rock frame as the shaft C is rocked back and forth by its hand crank C^2, and thus lower and raise the rock-frame.

The means employed to transmit the reciprocating action of the universal actuator to such denominational actuators as may be unlatched by key depression, consists of a series of spring-pressed arc-shaped levers D^1, pivoted to the rock-frame bar a², which bear against a pin b² fixed in the front arm of the denominational actuators.

Each of the levers D¹, is provided with a notch y, which serves on the downward action of the rock-frame to engage the pins b², of the denominational actuators and draw down with them such actuators as have been unlatched by key depression and to pass over the pins of such actuators as have not been unlatched.

When in the course of such downward movement the denominational actuators are intercepted by the stop-wires C¹, the yielding spring pressure of the levers D¹, allow the notches y, to slip over the pins b², and leave the denominational actuators and their type-wheels set for recording the item thus set up.

The means provided for impression of the type is shown in other drawings of a patent not reproduced here. The means provided consisted of a universal platen, which, the specification states, serves to press the ink-ribbon and paper against the type after all the figures of each item were set.

While Barbour, Baldwin and Pottin all used the universal platen to print the collective setting of type represented in the items or totals, as the case may be, each varied somewhat in detail. Baldwin used a toggle to press the platen toward the type, while Burroughs used a spring to press the platen against the type and a toggle to press it away from the type.

Burroughs claimed to have combined in his invention the printing of the totals, with the printing of the items, each of which it has been shown was claimed by the patentees of previous inventions but had not been combined in one machine prior to the Burroughs attempt.

The process for recording these totals in the Burroughs patent consisted of utilizing the action of the total wheels during their resetting or zeroizing movement to gauge the setting of the typewheels.

The specification shows that, during the downward motion or setting of the denominational actuators, as they set the type wheels, the numeral wheels are out of gear and receive no motion therefrom; and that after the recording of each item and during the return motion of denominational actuators, the numeral or total wheels are revolved forward in their accumulative action of adding the items and thus registering the total.

Provision is made, however, when it is desired to print the totals, to cause the totalizing wheels to enmesh with the denominational actuators on their downward or setting movement, and for the unlatching of all the racks so that by operating the hand lever C^5, the downward action of the racks will reverse the action of the totalizing wheels, which will revolve backward until the zeros show at the visible reading point, where they will be arrested by stops provided for that purpose. By this method the forward rotation accumulated on each wheel will, through the reverse action of zeroizing, give a like degree of action to the type-wheels through the denominational actuators. Thus the registration of the total wheels, it is claimed, will be transferred to the type-wheels and the record printed thereof as a footing to the column of numerical items that have been added.

To pass judgment on the recording machines of the patents that have been described, from the invention of Barbour to that of Burroughs, demands consideration, first, as to whether in any of the machines of these patents the primary features of legible recording were present.

All early arithmetical printing devices impractical

The question as to operativeness respecting other features is of no consideration until it is proven that the means disclosed for recording was practical. As non-recording adding or calculating machines they were not of a type that could compete with the more speedy key-driven machines dealt with in the preceding chapters; therefore without the capacity for legible recording, these patents must stand as representing a nonentity or as statutory evidence of the ineffective efforts of those who conceived the scheme of their makeup and attempted to produce a recording-adding machine.

Without the capacity for legible recording, of what avail is it that the machine of one of these patents should disclose advantages over another? It may be conceded that there are features set forth in the Pottin and Burroughs patents that if operatively combined with legible recording would disclose quite an advanced state of the Art at the time they were patented. But credit for such an operative combination cannot be given until it exists.

There is no desire to question the ingenuity displayed by any of these inventors, but in seeking the first practical recording-adding or calculating machine we must first find an operative machine of that type; one which will record in a practical and legible manner regardless of its other qualifications.

Practical method for recording disclosed later

The fact that the fundamental principle used for the impression of the type in the practical recorder of today is not displayed in any of these inventions, raises the question as to the effective operativeness of the printing scheme disclosed in the patents of these early machines.

In each of the four alleged recording-adding machine patents described, it will be noted that the means employed for printing was that of pressing the paper against the group of type by means of a universal platen or plate.

While with such a combination it may be possible to provide a set pressure great enough to legibly print a numerical item or total having eight to ten figures through an ink ribbon, it would not be practical to use the same pressure to print a single-digit figure, as it would cause the type to break through the paper. And yet in the numerical items and totals that have to be recorded in machines of the class under consideration, such wide variation is constantly encountered.

We are all familiar with the typewriter and the legible printing it produces. But suppose instead of printing each letter separately the whole word should be printed at once by a single-key depression, then, of course, single-letter words, such as the article "a" or the pronoun "I" would also have to be printed by a single-key depression. In this supposition we find a parallel of the requirements of a recording-adding machine.

If it were possible to so increase the leverage of the typewriter keys enough to cause a word of ten letters to be printed as legibly as a single letter is now printed, ten times the power would have to be delivered at the type-head. Then think what

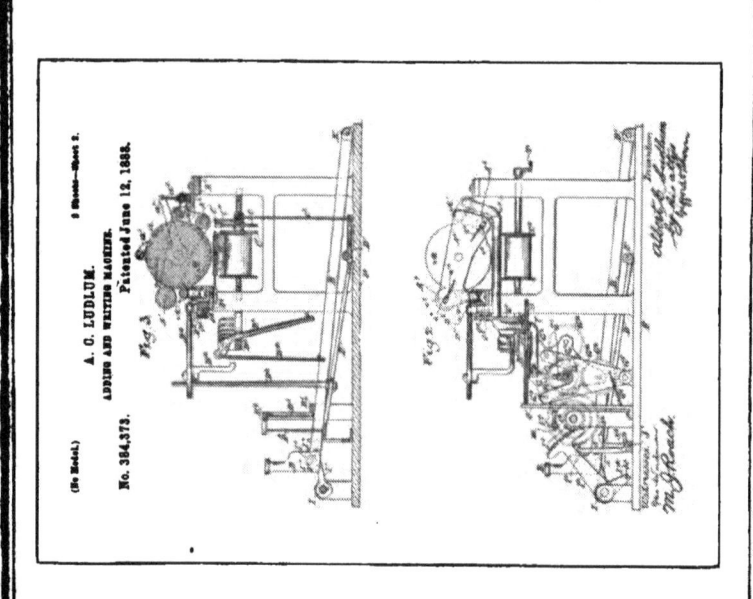

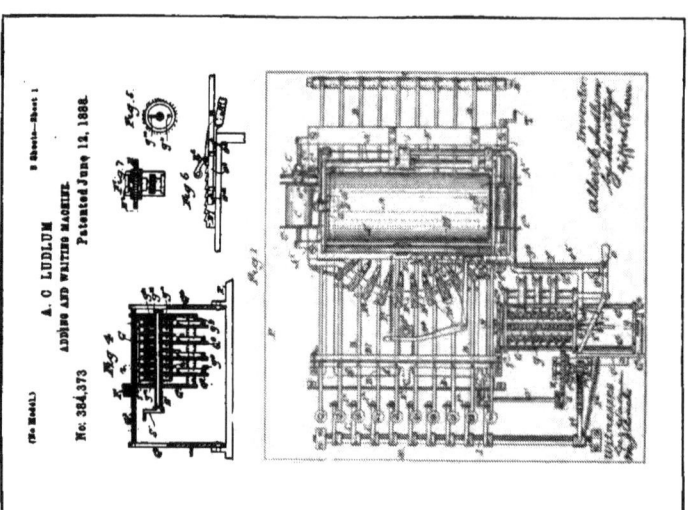

Drawings of Ludlum Patent No. 384,373

would happen with that same amount of power applied to print the letter "a," or letter "I." You would not question that under such conditions the type would break a hole in the paper. And yet the patentees of the said described inventions wanted the public to believe that their inventions were operative. But to be operative as recording-adding machines, they must meet such variable conditions as described.

Inoperative features of early recording mechanism

It is useless to believe that a variation of from one to ten or more type could be printed by a set amount of pressure through an ink-ribbon and be legible under all circumstances.

While the needle-type of Pottin may have printed the items legibly enough for a cash-register, it would not serve the purpose of a record for universal use. The use of regular type and the inking ribbon proposed in his specification would bring it within the inoperative features named.

The Ludlum Machine

In 1888, about two months prior to the issue of the Burroughs recording machine patent just referred to, a patent was issued to A. C. Ludlum for an adding and writing-machine. (See illustration on opposite page.)

It will be noted by reference to the drawings that the scheme is that of a typewriter with an adding mechanism attached.

Adding mechanism attached to typewriter

The details of the typewriter may be omitted, as most of us are familiar with typewriters. A feature that differed from the regular typewriter, however, was that the machine printed figures only and the carriage operated in the opposite direction, thus printing from right to left instead of left to right.

Description of Ludlum machine

A series of numeral wheels and their devices for the transfer of the tens, designed to register the totals, are shown mounted in a shiftable frame connected with the bar marked F, with the typewriter carriage, and is claimed to move therewith.

Each numeral wheel is provided with a gear marked G, which, as the carriage moves after writing or printing each figure of the item, is supposed to slide into mesh one at a time with an adding gear marked H, the engagement taking place from right to left. Or beginning with the right or units numeral wheel a higher order numeral wheel gear is supposed to shift through movement of the carriage into engagement with the adding gear H, each time a key is depressed.

The adding gear H, is supposed to receive varying degrees of rotation from the keys according to their numerical marking and to rotate the numeral wheel with which it happens to be engaged, a corresponding number of its ten marked points of registration.

Between the adding gear H, and the keys which act to drive it, is a ratchet and gear device consisting of the ratchet pawl pivoted to the adding gear H, the ratchet I^e, and its pinion gear, the segment gear I^3 fast to the rock shaft I, the nine arms I^1 fast to the rock shaft and the pins I^2, which are arranged in the key levers to contact with and depress the arms I^1 of the rock shaft varying distances, according to the value of the key depressed. That is, supposing that the full throw of the key-lever was required to actuate the rock shaft with its gear and ratchet connection to give nine-tenths of a revolution to the numeral wheel in adding the digit nine, the pin I^2 in the (9) key-lever would in that case be in contact with its arm I^1, of the rock shaft, but the pins I^2, of each of the other key levers would be arranged to allow lost motion before the pin should engage its arm I^1 of the rock shaft, in accordance with the difference of their adding value.

According to the specification, Ludlum evidently had the idea that he could stop the adding gear H, while under the high rate of speed it would receive from a quick depression of a key, by jabbing the detent J between the fine spacing of the gear teeth shown in his drawing. But to those familiar with the possibility of such stop devices, its inoperativeness will be obvious; not that the principle properly applied would not work, for its application by Felt prior to that of Ludlum proved the possibilities of this method of gauging additive actuation.

The detent lever J, as shown in the drawings, is operated by the hinged plate D, through action of the key levers, as any one of them are depressed.

Under depression of a key, the hinged plate D, being carried down with it, engages the arm J^2 of the detent and throws the tooth at its upper end into the teeth of the gear H.

The timing of the entry of the tooth of the detent is supposed to be gauged to enter the right tooth, but as the action of these parts is fast, slow or medium at the will of the operator, considerable time must be allowed for variation in the entry of the detent tooth, which requires space, as certain parts will fly ahead under the sudden impact they may receive from a quick stroke, where they would not under a slow stroke, but no allowance was provided for such contingency.

The means provided for the carry of the tens consist of the gears G^9, meshing with the numeral wheel gears and the single gear tooth g^9, attached to it, which, at each revolution of the lower wheel, as it passes from 9 to 0, engages the gear of the numeral wheel of higher denomination and was supposed to turn the higher gear one-tenth of a revolution, thus registering one greater.

On account of the Gears G^9, of one order and the gear tooth g^9, of another order operating on the same numeral wheel gear, the transfer gears are arranged alternately on separate shafts, one at the side and one below the numeral wheels.

Ludlum machine inoperative

The mechanical scheme disclosed in the Ludlum patent, to the unsophisticated may seem to be operative. But to those familiar with the Art of key-driven adding mechanism it will at once be obvious that even if the typewriter feature was constructed properly the possibility of correctly adding the items as they were printed was absolutely impossible.

Laying aside several other features of inoperativeness, obvious to those who know such mechanism, the reader, although not versed in the Art of key-driven adding mechanism, will observe from the preceding chapter, that the means provided for transferring the tens without any control for the numeral wheels against over-rotation, would make correct addition impossible.

The drawings and specification of the Ludlum patent disclose a mere dream and show that they were not copied from the make-up of an operative machine.

It was a daring scheme and one that none but a dreamer would undertake to construct in the method shown. There have in later years been some successful ten-key recording machines made and sold, but they were of a very different design and principle.

There have also been several adding attachments made and sold that could be adjusted to a regular commercial typewriter that are claimed to be dependable, but none of these machines were early enough to be claimed as the first operative recording-adding machine, or the first adding machine in which the principle used for the legible recording of the numerical items used in the machines of today may be found.

First Practical Recorders

THE fact that Barbour, Baldwin, Pottin, Ludlum and Burroughs attempted to produce a recording-adding machine shows that as far back as 1872, and at periods down to 1888, there was at least in the minds of these men a conception of the usefulness of such a machine, and the fact that there were five with the same thought is fairly good evidence of the need for a machine of this class.

In some of the human-interest articles issued through the advertising department of the Burroughs Adding Machine Co. it is stated that Wm. Seward Burroughs was a bank clerk prior to his efforts at adding-machine construction. It is conceivable, therefore, that his first efforts at adding-machine invention should be directed toward the production of a machine that would be of service in the bank for the bringing together of the loose items of account that are to be found in the form of checks, drafts, and the like, by printing a record of the items and their totals during the process of adding them together.

Burroughs a bank clerk

It is not surprising, therefore, that a manufacturer of a successful calculating machine should, through his contact with the trade, come to the conclusion that there was use for a machine of this class in the banks. As proof of this, we find that an application for a recording-adding machine

Felt interested in recorder Art

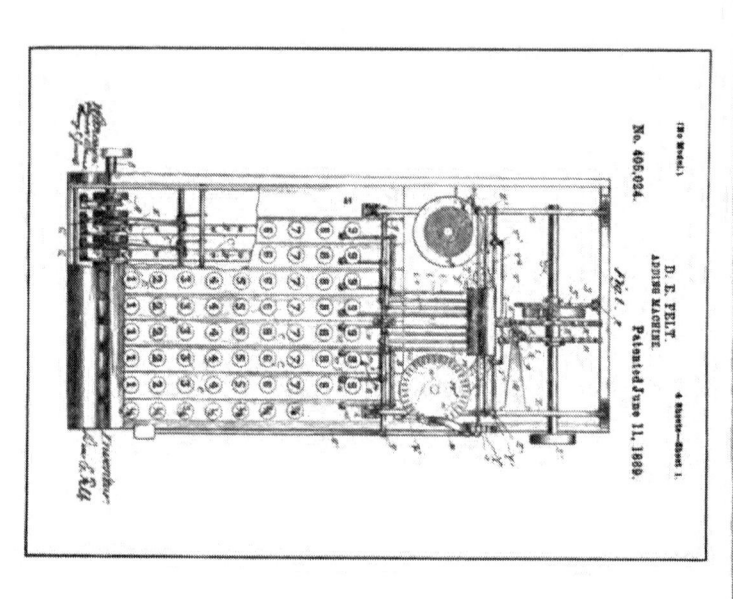

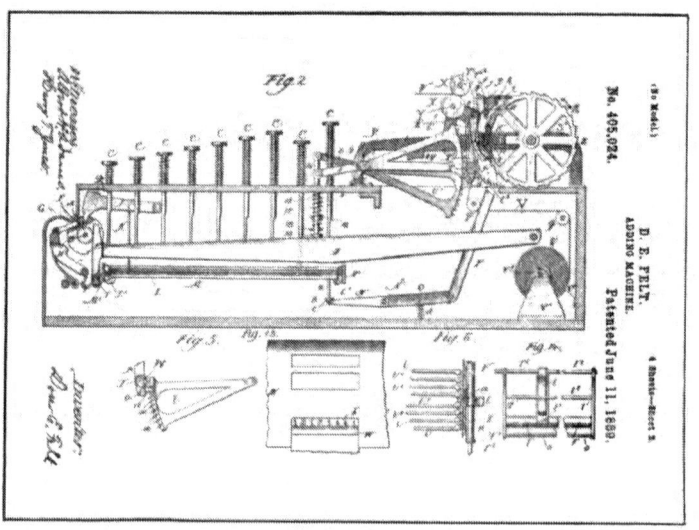

From Drawings of Felt Patent No. 405,024

patent was filed January 19, 1888, by D. E. Felt, which was allowed and issued June 11, 1889.

Some of the drawings of this patent will be found reproduced on the opposite page, from which the reader will note that Felt combined his scheme for recording with the mechanism of the machine he was then manufacturing and selling under the trade name of "Comptometer." *Felt's first recording machine*

In this patent is shown the first application of the type sector combined with the individual type impression for printing the figures of the items as they were added, thus giving equal impression, whether there were one or a dozen figures in the item or total to be printed.

While the average mechanical engineer would not at a glance recognize any great advantage in placing the type figures directly on the sector instead of using the type-wheel and segment gear to drive it, as shown in two of the previously described patents, there is plenty of evidence of its advantage in the fact that all the later successful inventors have followed the Felt scheme. It provided more simple construction for the narrow space these parts must occupy for practical linear spacing.

As the adding mechanism of this machine corresponds to that of the Felt patent 371,496, previously described in the preceding chapter, it is not necessary to duplicate the description here. Suffice it to say, that by the depression of a key in any order, the value of that key is added to the numeral wheel of that order, and if the figure added is great enough when added to that previously registered on the wheel, a ten will be transferred to the higher wheel by a carrying mechanism specially provided to allow the said higher wheel *Felt recording mechanism combined with his calculating machine* being in turn operated by an ordinal series of keys, thus providing the means whereby a series of denominational orders of key-driven adding mechanism may be interoperative.

Description of Felt's first recorder

In Fig. 2 of the drawings is shown the result of striking the (8) key, which may be considered illustrative of such action in any order, whether units, tens, hundreds, thousands, etc.

The depression of the (8) key is shown to have carried the lever D down eight of its nine additive points of movement, causing the plunger 15, bearing against its upper edge, to drop with it under the action of the plunger spring 17.

To the upper end of this plunger, is pivotally attached an arm of the type sector U, which is in turn pivoted to the rod y, and by the lowering of the plunger 15, is rocked on its pivot, raising the type-head until the number (8) type is presented opposite the printing bar or platen T, which is hung on the pivot arms T^1, so that it may be swung forward and backward.

An ink-ribbon w, and its shifting mechanism is provided, as shown in Fig. 1; the paper v, is supplied in ribbon form from a roll and passes between the ink-ribbon and the platen T.

Normally, the platen, the paper and the ink-ribbon are in a retracted position, allowing space for the type sector to raise and lower freely. But, as shown in Fig. 2, a type impression is taking place through the escapement of the cam wheel R^1, which is located back of the platen, and which, as shown, has forced the cam lever 1 forward, pressing the spring p, against the platen T, thus forcing the paper and ribbon forward against the type, and printing the figure 8.

After the cam-tooth passes, the platen, paper, ink-ribbon and spring return to normal, allowing the type sector freedom to drop when the key is released.

The cam wheel R is propelled by a spring S (Fig. 1), wound by the hand-knob S^3, and is released for action through the escapement of the pallet wheel R attached to the cam wheel R and the pallet c.

The pallet c is tripped each time a key is depressed and is shown in the tripped position operated by the link P and the plural-armed lever O, N, which through its manifold arms N, may receive action through pins a, of any of the rock bars L, as they are depressed by the keys.

The cycle of action described takes place with every key depressed, except that the movement of the type sector varies according to the key depressed.

As the printing in this Felt invention was by individualized type impression, legibility of recording as well as accurate addition was obtained. Although this patent shows that Felt had produced such an operative combination, there are two features in this patent which would prevent its becoming a marketable machine.

First individualized type impression combined with printing sector

One of these features was that of having to wind the motor spring that furnished power for the type impression. The other feature was that there was no provision for printing the ciphers. Although the ciphers were always omitted from the keyboard of non-recording adders, as they could perform no function in addition or other forms of calculation, they could not without inconvenience, be eliminated from items in recording.

The Second Felt Recorder

First practical arithmetical recorder

While the last-described Felt patent was still pending, Felt improved his mechanism for recording, installing new features and eliminating the objectionable features referred to. These improvements were of such a satisfactory nature that the Felt & Tarrant Mfg. Co. made twenty-five recording-adders, with the new features, which were sold to various banks. The first of these machines was placed on trial with the Merchants & Manufacturers National Bank of Pittsburgh, Pa., in December of 1889.

Good evidence of the practical features of this machine was set forth in a testimonial given at the time by W. A. Shaw, the cashier of the bank, after it had been given a six months' test. This testimonial is extant and has been reproduced on opposite page.

The first sale of a recording-adding machine on record

Records show that the bank purchased that "Comptograph," which was the trade name given the Felt recording-adder, and used it until 1899, at which time this machine, along with others of the same make purchased at a later date, were replaced by the bank with "Comptographs" of more modern type.

This Felt recording machine was without question the first practical recording-adding machine ever sold that would produce legible printed records of items and totals under the variable conditions that have to be met in such a class of recording.

After ten years of service this first practical recording-adding machine was still in excellent condition, and in 1907 was secured by the Comptograph Co. from the Bank of Pittsburgh, into which the Merchants & Manufacturers National Bank,

Merchants & Manufacturers National Bank
Capital $800,000.

Pittsburgh, June 11, 1890

Felt & Tarrant Manfg Co.
52 Illinois St
Chicago Ills

Gentlemen

This Bank has in use a Comptometer and a Comptograph, the former has been in use more than a year, the latter about six months. We would not do without either of these machines. The Comptograph is invaluable where long lists of items are required with the footings to be made. The saving in time and tedious mental labor is very great.

It is not more difficult to use than a type writing machine, hardly as much so, to most persons.

Resp.
[signature]

Testimonial

Felt Recording and Listing Machine.
Purchased and Used for Ten Years by the Merchants & Manufacturers Bank of Pittsburgh, Pa.
Machine is now in the National Museum at Washington

along with other banks, had been merged. It was finally procured by Mr. Felt and presented to the National Museum of Washington, D. C., where it may now be found on exhibit along with other inventions produced by Felt. A photo reproduction of this machine as it appeared before it was presented to the Museum, is shown on the opposite page.

Features of first practical recorder — Like the machine of the first Felt recorder patent, it was a visible printer, each figure being printed as the key was depressed, the paper being shifted by the hand lever shown at the right.

Unlike the former machine, however, the operator was not called upon to perform the extra operation of winding up a spring to furnish power for the printing.

Power for the printing was stored by the action of the paper shift-lever and an entirely different printing device was used. Provision for printing the ciphers automatically was also a feature of this machine. It was not necessary to operate cipher keys, and there were no such keys to be operated. To print an item having ciphers in it required only the omission of the ciphers as the ciphers would automatically fill in.

The arrangement of the paper shows a good improvement over the first machine, as it was more accessible, being fed from a roll at the top down and around rolls below and looped back so that it is moved upward on the printed surface, where it may be torn off as desired.

The mechanism of this machine is not illustrated in any one patent. The Felt patents Nos. 441,233 and 465,255 cover the new feature, but the later patent, No. 465,255, shows it best. Some of the drawings of the last-named patent are reproduced on the opposite page to help in explanation of the details of the new features.

Description of Felt's second recorder

By referring to the drawings, it will be noted that the form of the front of the casing differs from the machine. Other drawings of the patent, not shown here, disclose features of still later invention than were in the machine of the photo reproduction. But it is with the printing device that we are now interested, and it was in this patent that it was first shown in the form used in the first marketed machine referred to.

The type sector marked 81 is like that of the first patent, except that it is provided with the ciphers as well as the nine digits.

The cipher type are always presented for printing when the sectors are resting at normal. Thus, if an impression can be made without depressing the keys in that order, a cipher will be printed, as will be shown later.

Back of the paper and pivoted to the rod 97, are a series of printing hammers 87, one for each type sector.

The hammers are operated by the spring 88, and are shown retained against the tension of their springs by the trigger latches 89.

These trigger latches are pivoted on the fixed shaft 171[a], and actuated by the springs 92 to cause their engagement with the notch 90 of the printing hammers.

Each of the trigger latches are provided with a laterally extending lug 93, formed on their lower arm, and each lug overlaps the back of the lower arm of the adjacent trigger latch to the right of it, so that if any trigger latch should be operated

From Drawings of Felt Patent No. 465,255

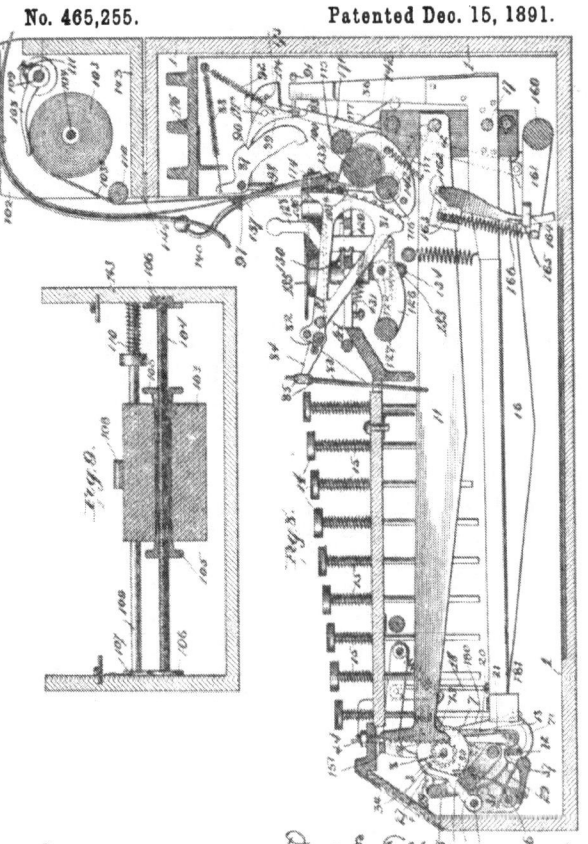

so as to extricate it from the notch 50 of its printing hammer, its overlapping lug 93, would cause a like action of the trigger latch to the right of that, and so on; thus releasing all the trigger latches to the right of the latch originally released. Such releasing, of course, allowed the printing-hammers 87, to spring forward in all the orders so affected.

The long-stop actuating lever marked 16, corresponds with the lever G of the Felt key-driven calculator shown in a preceding chapter, and performs the same function as the rock bars L of the first Felt recorder patent. These stop levers 16 are pivoted at 17, and are provided with rear arms 86, extending upward with their ends opposite the lateral extending lug 93, of the trigger latch, which corresponds to the order of keys which the lever 16 serves.

In the rear upwardly-extending end of each of these levers 16, an adjusting screw 91, is provided as a tappet for tripping the trigger latch corresponding to its order.

From the above-described combination of mechanism, it may be seen that if a key in any order is depressed, it will, as it comes in contact with the stop lever 16, not only cause the adding mechanism to be stopped through the stop 19, but it will also, through its rear arm 86, cause the trigger latch of its order to trip, and likewise all the trigger latches and printing-hammers to the right, thus printing the figure presented on the printing sector in the order in which the key was operated and the ciphers in the orders to the right in case the keys in the order to the right have not previously been operated.

The individual presentation of the type figures upon key depression, except for the ciphers which were normally presented for printing, required that in striking the keys, to give correct recording of the items, the operation must be from right to left. That is, for example, if the item to be added was $740.85, the operator would depress the (5) key in the units cents column, the (8) key in the tens of cents column; the cipher in the units dollars column would be omitted, the (4) key in the tens of dollars, and the (7) key in the hundreds of dollars column would be struck.

The printing hammers were provided with means for resetting after being tripped in the recording action. This means is connected with the paper shift-lever, so that as the paper was shifted or fed upward, ready for recording the next item, the printing-hammers were all reset and latched on their respective trigger latches, ready for a new item.

Fixed to the shaft 97, on which the printing-hammers are pivoted, is a bail, marked 98, part of which is shown in the drawing, the horizontal bar of which normally lies under and out of the way of the hammers as they plunge forward in printing. And attached to the right-hand end of the shaft 97, is a crank arm connected by a link to the paper-shift hand-lever, which may be seen on the right in the photo reproduction of the machine. This connection is arranged so that depressing the lever causes the shaft 97 to rock the bail 98 rearward, thus picking up any tripped printing-hammers and relatching them.

The totals had to be printed, as in the first-described Felt recorder, by depressing a key corresponding in value to the figure showing on the wheel in each order.

Felt principle of printing adopted by all manufacturers of recorders

The principle involved in the individual hammer-blow, combined with the ordinal type sector for recording in a recording-adder was new, and was the feature that has made the adding-recording machine of today possible, as is well in evidence by the presence of this combination in all the recorders that have been made by the successful manufacturers of listing or recording-adding and calculating machines. Some manufacturers have substituted a vertical moving type bar for the pivoted sector, but the scheme is the same, as the purpose is to get the arrangement of the type in columnar order, and does not change the fundamental features of the combination which furnished the practical means for the individual type impression.

THE FELT TABULATOR

Wide paper carriage for tabulating

The next feature in the Art, that has served in the make-up of the up-to-date recorders, was the wide paper-carriage. This feature will probably be recognized by many as a means supplied for the recording of columns of items in series on sheet-paper.

As will be noted, roll-paper in ribbon form had been used in all the previously illustrated and described recorders. While the Ludlum patent shows a carriage, it had no capacity for handling more than a single column of numerical items. The carriage in the Ludlum machine was a feature necessary to the typewriter construction and offered no solution to the feature of tabulating.

The first disclosure of the wide carriage feature for tabulating was in a machine made by D. E. Felt

Felt Tabulator

in 1889, which he exhibited to the U. S. Census Bureau at Washington, D. C., in 1890. The machine was also exhibited at the World's Fair in Chicago, in 1893, along with other products in this line of the Felt & Tarrant Mfg. Co. A photo reproduction of this machine is shown on opposite page. *The wide paper carriage machine*

The machine was left at the Census Bureau, where it was used for several weeks, and was very much liked. Felt made a contract to furnish ten machines of this type, and the machine was recommended for purchase by G. K. Holmes, Special Agent of the Census Bureau, but like many other government department requisitions, the purchase order was never issued.

Although this feature is now found in all first-class recording-adders, the recording machine Art was too new in 1890 for the new feature to be appreciated, and was not pushed, as there seemed to be no demand for the wide carriage then. On this account Felt delayed applying for a patent on his invention until 1899.

In 1904 a license under the patent was granted the Burroughs Adding Machine Co., but soon after the granting of the license another manufacturer of recording-adders brought out a machine with a wide carriage, which was the start of a series of long-drawn-out infringement suits. The fact that Felt had delayed taking out his patent formed the grounds on which the Court finally decided that Felt, from lack of diligence in applying for a patent, had abandoned his invention, which made it public property. *Litigation on tabulator patents*

The tags which may be seen tied to the carriage of the machine are the official tags used to identify it as a court exhibit during the long term of years the suits were pending in litigation.

Outside of the tabulating scheme, the machine was in other respects the same as the recorder just described as the roll-paper "Comptograph."

"Cross Tabulating"

The paper, as may be noted, is held in a shiftable carriage and is operated by two levers, one to feed the paper vertically and reset the printing-hammers, while the other moved the carriage laterally for the spacing of the columns of items or the cross-printing when desired. Besides the lever action for shifting and paper-feeding, means were provided on the right-hand end of the carriage for performing these functions; one of these is the thumb knob which served to feed the sheet of paper into the rolls; the other is a small lever which allows the operator to shift the carriage by hand independent of the carriage shift-lever.

THE THIRD FELT RECORDER

While the first lot of recording-adders manufactured by Felt were wholly practical, as was well proved by the statements of those who purchased them, it is easy to pick out features in their make-up that today, when compared with the new highly-developed Art, would seem to make them impractical.

The necessity of operating from right to left and the necessity of printing the totals by key depression were features that, in view of there being nothing better in those days, did not seem objectionable to those who used them. They were features, however, that Felt overcame and eliminated in the next lot of machines manufactured and placed on the market in 1890.

This lot of machines, one hundred in number (a goodly number in those days), were equipped with a special hand-knob in front on the left side for

FELT'S COMPTOGRAPH.

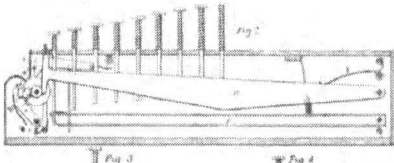

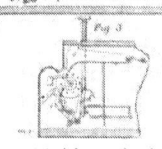

Every one who has had any practice in the use of an arithmometer of the ordinary type will recognise that a considerable loss of time results from the necessity of setting the slides to the proper numbers. The machine which we illustrate on this page is free from this cause of loss, as the slides are replaced by a set of keys like those of a typewriter, having figured knobs. The touching of any one of these knobs adds the corresponding number to the total shown by the indicating wheels. Fig. 1 is a perspective view of the machine showing the keyboard. Each knob, it will be seen, is lettered with two letters, one set being used in subtracting and the other in adding. Fig. 2 shows a section through one row of keys, of which it should be observed there are only nine, the cypher being omitted. These keys depress to a greater or less extent a long lever a which is L shaped in section, and is pivoted on a shaft running across the machine from side to side at the back, a spring b retaining it to position when the pressure is taken off the keys. At the end of this lever is a segmental rack gearing into a small pinion, which rotates on a second horizontal shaft and turns it to a greater or less extent. This pinion has attached to it a disc shown in Figs. 8 and 9 and also in Fig. 5. This disc carries a pawl c, Fig. 8, which engages with the teeth of a ten toothed ratchet wheel E. Fig. 2, and moves it round a distance corresponding to the key struck. The ratchet wheel is firmly fastened to the registering wheel which, as shown in Fig. 1, carries the different digits on its periphery, and indicates the result of any operation as an ordinary counter. Exceptional care has been taken to insure the accuracy of the registration; the devices for this purpose we will now describe. Any backward motion of the registering wheel is prevented by a pawl d, Figs. 3 and 4. But the when it moreover, when at rest, locked as regards forward motion, and is only free to rotate when the lever corresponding to it is depressed, or if a unit is to be carried over from the wheel behind it. This locking is accomplished by a pawl. Figs 3 and 4, which when at rest engages with the teeth of the number wheel, as in Fig. 3. It carries, however, a pin which when the machine is at rest lies in the notch cut in the rim of the disc already mentioned, as shown in Figs. 8 and 9. When a key is depressed this disc is rotated and the pin attached in the pawl slides up the inclined part of the notch, and so frees the number wheel, which can then be rotated by the pawl c, as already described. It will be seen that there is a good deal of lost motion before this pawl engages with the teeth; this is done so as to allow time for the stop motion pawl e to get clear. Hence, in depressing a key, the disc is put in rotation by the pinion As it rotates it first frees the number wheel pawl which locks it, and then moves it forward a distance by the pawl c. To insure that this shall not be rotated too much on depression, a second mechanism is used. It will be seen that the stalks of the keys are prolonged down the of the key spindles are arranged and also pivoted at the back of the case is a lever n, and that below this lever this lever f, when they strike, above of motion, thus depressing its for

One of the Early "Comptographs"

automatically printing the totals, and with means by which the ciphers were printed only on operation of the paper shift-lever, which allowed the operator to depress the keys from left to right or any way he pleased.

The best evidence as to what these machines looked like is to be found in the reproduction on the opposite page of an illustration which appeared in "Engineering" of London, in 1891.

Felt recorder in "Engineering" of London, Eng.

It will be noted that the patent drawings of the Felt calculator are also displayed. They were used to describe the adding mechanism of the recorder.

The total printing device is shown and described in patent No. 465,255, while the patent for the printing of the ciphers by the hand shift-lever was not applied for until 1904.

It may be argued, and argued true, that these two later features in their generic application to the recording-adding machine Art were anticipated by Burroughs in his invention herein previously described. But, assuming that these features were operative features in the Burroughs machine, they could not be claimed in combination with a printing mechanism that was operative to give practical results and in themselves did not make the recording-adder possible. Nor was the means shown for recording the totals of use except with means for legible recording.

There is no desire to discredit what Burroughs did, but let the credit for what Burroughs accomplished come into its own, in accordance with the chronological order in which it may be proved that Burroughs really produced a machine that had a practical and legible recording mechanism. Then we will find that to produce such proof we must

Total recording a Felt combination

Legible listing of items and automatic recording of totals first achieved by Felt

accept the fact that in all the successful recording machines manufactured and sold by the Burroughs Adding Machine Co., the printing type-sector, the printing type-hammers and the overlapping hammer-triggers with their broad functioning features forming a part of Felt's invention, have been used to produce legible recording, and that the combination of practical total printing was dependent on Felt's achievement.

We might say that broadly Burroughs invented means that could be worked in combination with the Felt printing scheme to automatically print the totals, which is in evidence in all the practical machines put out by the Burroughs Co.

But such a combination was first produced by Felt in 1890, and was not produced by Burroughs until 1892.

As has been shown, Felt built his recording scheme into his key-driven calculating machine, and added the paper shifting-lever to furnish the power which was utilized finally for setting the printing-hammers and tripping them for the ciphers.

Such a combination divided the work, but made a two-motion machine, whereas the adding mechanism was designed on the one-motion principle. Now the principle of the two-motion machine was old, very old. The great Gottfried Leibnitz invented the first two-motion calculator in 1694. (See illustration on opposite page.)

The Leibnitz machine was a wonderful invention and there seems to be a question as to its operativeness. As a feature of historic interest, however, it created considerable commotion in scientific circles when exhibited to the Royal Society of London.

Gottfried Wilhelm Leibnitz

Leibnitz Calculator, made in 1694
The First Two-Motion Machine Designed to Compute
Multiplication by Repeated Addition

The first really practical machine of this type, however, was invented by a Frenchman named Charles Xavier Thomas, in 1820, and has since become known as the "Thomas Arithmometre."

The Thomas machine is made and sold by a number of different foreign manufacturers, and is used to a considerable extent in Europe and to a limited extent in the United States.

But two-motion calculators, from Leibnitz down to date, have always been constructed so that the primary or first action involved merely the setting of the controlling devices and performed no function in the supplying of power to operate the mechanism which does the adding. With such machines the load was thrown on to the secondary action.

The key-set principle more practical for recorders

This, of course, made the primary action of setting, a very light action, especially when keys came into use, and as there are several key depressions to each secondary or crank action, it may be understood that while the action of Felt's printing or paper shift-lever was light, the action of the keys which were called upon to perform most of the work was much harder than it would have been if his adding mechanism had been designed on the key-set crank-operated plan of the regular two-motion machine such as illustrated in the Pottin or Burroughs patents described.

Thus, when Burroughs applied the Felt recording principle to his key-set crank-operated adding mechanism, he produced a type of recording machine which proved to be more acceptable from an operative standpoint than the recorder made by Felt; and yet the writer has read testimonials given by those who had both the Felt key-driven

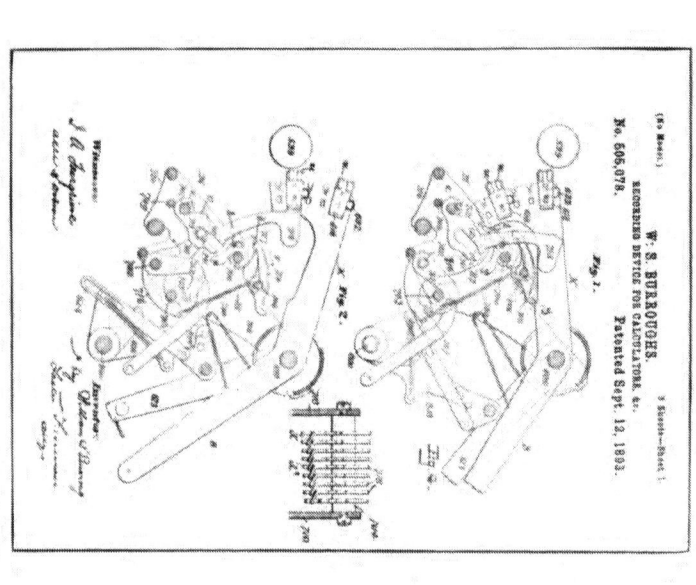

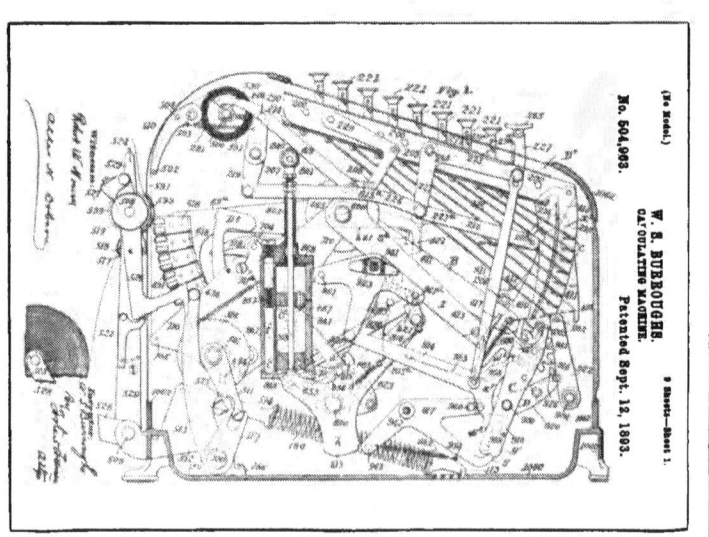

From Drawings of Burroughs' Patents
Nos. 504,963 and 505,078

recorder and the Burroughs key-set crank-operated recorders, who claimed they could see no advantage.

Probably the best proof lies in the fact that Felt finally abandoned the key-driven feature in his recorders, as may be noted from the later-day "Comptograph."

THE FIRST PRACTICAL BURROUGHS RECORDER

The first Burroughs patent to show the successful combination referred to was No. 504,963, applied for May 5, 1892, and issued September 12, 1893. The printing scheme, however, while indicated in the said patent, was applied for in a divisional patent, No. 505,078, issued on the same date. Drawings from both these patents are shown on opposite page.

The new printing device, as will be noted, instead of operating at the bottom of the machine, operates at the rear and prints the paper against a roll mounted outside of the casing.

Description of first practical Burroughs recorder

Outside of adopting the Felt method of printing, the general scheme of construction used in the machine of the former-described Burroughs patent was maintained, except that the levers D, used to drag the denominational actuators down, were omitted, and a series of springs, one for each actuator, was supplied to pull such levers down as are released by key-depression when the common actuator drops under crank action.

Thus the description previously given will suffice for a general understanding of the mechanical functions of the adding mechanism and the general scheme for the setting up of the type in these later patents.

The construction of the type sectors, the printing-hammers and the trigger-latches used to re-

Burroughs Recorder

tain the hammers against the action of their operating springs is best shown in the drawings of patent No. 505,078 on page 136. Fig. 1 shows the normal relation, while Fig. 2 illustrates the same mechanism in the act of printing.

The type sector as shown in drawings of patent No. 505,078 is marked K, while in the drawings of No. 504,963 it will be found marked 611ª. They are formed from a continuation of the denominational actuators for the total register in the same manner that the type-wheel gear-racks h, of the previously described Burroughs patent were formed.

The type u, are arranged on movable blocks marked 618, which are shown held in their retracted or normal position by springs 682, but when pressure is brought to bear against these type blocks in a direction outward from the sector, the spring 682 will give and the type blocks will slide outward in the slots provided to guide their action.

The paper, as will be noted, is fed from a roll, up between the type and the printing-roll 599, in the same manner as the paper of a typewriter, and through the interposition of an ink-ribbon between the type and the paper, the pressing of the type against the ink-ribbon, paper and roll gives imprint.

The pressure brought to bear on the type is through the hammer-blow of the printing-hammers 715, of which there is one for each ordinal printing sector. These hammers are pivoted to the rod 701, and are spring-actuated through the medium of the pin 741, the lever 716, and spring 780, which, combined with the cam-slot w, in the printing-hammers, serve to force the printing-hammers into the position shown in Fig. 2.

The printing-hammers are normally retracted and latched by a series of trigger latches 117, through the latch-tooth b, which engages the lever 716 at v.

Each trigger-latch 117, is pivoted on the rod 700, and provided with an overlapping lug as shown in Fig. 4. These overlapping lugs, like those described on the trigger-latches in the Felt patent, serve as an automatic means of filling in the ciphers in the same manner as described in the Felt machine.

The means for tripping the overlapping trigger latches naturally differed from the means shown in the Felt machine, as the Burroughs machine was not key-driven.

A very ingenious means for the tripping of the trigger-latches is shown, consisting of the dogs 718, and rock-frame 711, and tie-rods 703-704, which co-operate with a cam-shoulder y on the arm of the printing-sectors, to remain neutral or to disengage the trigger-latches through a reciprocating action, shown in dotted lines in Fig. 1, patent No. 505,078.

The tripping action takes place at the end of the forward motion of the actuating hand-crank through connections not shown in the drawings.

It may be understood that on account of the overlapping of the trigger-latches of the printing-hammers that if, as described in relation to the Felt recording-machine, one of the trigger-latches in any order to the left of the units order should be tripped, it would cause all the trigger-latches to the right to be also tripped, and the printing-hammers thus released to spring forward, giving an individual hammer-blow for each type impression.

Thus, if the five-hundred-dollar key should be depressed, only the trigger latch in that order need be tripped. This is brought about through the fact that normally the tripping-dogs 718 are held out of tripping engagement by the cam surface y of the type-sector, as the rock-frame in which the dogs are mounted is moved forward in its tripping action. But as the hundred-dollar order type-sector has been lifted through the setting of the (5) key in that order, it allows the tripping-dog to engage the trigger-latch of that order, and through the overlapping feature of the trigger-latches to trip and print the ciphers to the right.

It will be noted that the application of the printing-hammers varied in detail from that of Felt much the same as placing the latch on the gate post instead of on the gate. In the generic principle, however, the individual hammer-blow for each individual impression was maintained.

Date of use of first practical Burroughs recorder

There have been many conflicting statements made regarding the date of the first Burroughs listing or recording machine, which is probably due to the fact that the statements were not qualified by such terms as "practically operative" or "legible recording."

Dates given as that of the first Burroughs recording machine range from 1884 to 1892. In a book published by the Burroughs Co. in 1912, under the title of the "Book of the Burroughs," there was a statement that the first practical machines were made in 1891.

H. B. Wyeth, at one time sales agent for the Burroughs Co., and whose father was president

First in Use (1892)

First in Usefulness in Over 300 Different Lines of Business

First in the Hearts of Over 63,000 Users

The Burroughs Adding and Listing Machine

¶ Here's where 1908 finds the adding-machine industry.

¶ We sold 13,314 machines in 1907.

¶ This one year's sales of BURROUGHS machines is greater than the **combined** sales of **all other** makes of adding and listing machines during **all** the years of their existence - and some of them have been on the market nearly as long as the BURROUGHS.

¶ "All other makes" includes some twenty or more different styles of adding and listing machines which have made their bid for public favor since the perfection of the adding and listing machine by William Seward Burroughs fifteen years ago. Many of these other devices have now passed into adding-machine history. Some of them were well financed and ably organized, yet they failed to win the endorsement of commercial success. Surely there was some fault in the machines themselves which made them unfitted to compete with the known reliability of the BURROUGHS.

¶ Regarding those machines which have survived, there are more BURROUGHS in use to-day in a single State than any other maker of adding and listing machines has sold in the whole United States.

¶ The BURROUGHS **sold** more machines in a single State in 1907 than some of its leading competitors **produced** in the same period.

¶ These facts indicate the place which the BURROUGHS occupies in the estimation of the purchasing public.

There are 58 Different Styles of BURROUGHS---One Built for Every Line of Business

63,574 Burroughs Users (Jan. 18, '08)

Burroughs Adding Machine Company

67 Amsterdam Avenue, Detroit, Michigan, U. S. A.

From the February 1908 Issue of
Office Appliances Magazine

of the company in 1891 and several years thereafter, testified in court that the first sale of a Burroughs recording machine was made about December, 1892. Corroboration of his testimony is set forth in a Burroughs advertisement which appeared in the February number of Office Appliances Magazine in 1908, a reproduction of which is shown on the opposite page.

That Burroughs was experimenting as early as 1885 is no doubt correct; and that in this respect he antidated Felt's first attempt to produce a recording-adder, is not questioned. But when it comes to the question of who produced the first practical recording-adder, there is no room for doubt in face of the evidence at hand.

Introduction of the Modern Accounting Machine

AS the reader has been carried along through the tangle of mechanical efforts of the men who have racked their brains to produce means that would relieve the burden of those who have to juggle with arithmetical problems and masses of figures in the day's accounting, there was one phase of subject that has not been touched upon. While these inventors were doing their best to benefit mankind and, without doubt, with the thought of reaping a harvest for themselves, the public, who could have been the prime beneficiary, did not hasten to avail themselves of the opportunity.

Opposition to the use of machines for accounting

In the early days, when the key-driven calculator was marketed, and later when the recording-adder was also placed on the market, the efforts of the salesmen for each of these types of machines, in their endeavor to interest possible purchasers, were met with anything but enthusiasm. Of course, now and then a wide-awake businessman was willing to be shown and would purchase, but ninety-nine out of the hundred who really had use for a machine of either type could not at that early date be awakened to the fact.

Although the calculator and the recording-adder are indispensable factors in business today, and have served to improve the lot of the book-keeper and those employed in expert accounting in general, they met with very strong opposition for the first few years from employers of this class. It was strongly evident that the efforts of bookkeepers and counting-house clerks to prevent these machines entering their department were inspired by the fear that it would displace their services and interfere with their chance of a livelihood.

Again, men of this class, and even those in charge of large departments, took the mere suggestion that they had use for a calculator or recording-adder as an insult to their efficiency, and would almost throw the salesman out. Others would very politely look the machine over and tell the salesman what a wonderful machine it was, but when asked to give the machine a trial, they would immediately back up and say that they had absolutely no use for such a machine; whereas possibly now the same department is using twenty-five to a hundred such machines.

Of the two classes of machines, the recording, or listing machines, as they are commonly called, although a later product, were the first to sell in quantities that may be called large sales. This was probably due to the fact that they were largely sold to the banks, who have always been more liberal in recognizing the advantages of labor-saving devices than any other class of business. *Banks more liberal in recognition*

The presence of these machines in the bank also had a tendency to influence business-men to install recorders where the key-driven calculator would have given far greater results in quantity of work and expense of operating. In these days, however, the average business-man is alive to his requirements, and selects what is best suited to his needs instead of being influenced by seeing a machine used by others for an entirely different purpose. The theory of using the printed list of items as a means of checking back has blown into a bubble and burst, and the non-lister has come into its own, not but what there has always been a good sale for these machines except for the first four years.

Improvements slow for first few years

On account of the years it took to educate business into the use of these two types of accounting machines, and the fact that the sales of both were small at first, there were few improvements for several years, as improvements depend upon prosperity.

Such changes as have been made since were largely aimed at refinements, but there are some very noteworthy features added to the performance of both types of machines, which are explained and described in following chapters, where the subject will be treated under the class of machines they affect.

The High-Speed Calculator

The High-Speed Calculator

AS previously stated, the calculating machine was old when Felt improved the Art by combining the key-drive with a plurality of co-operative orders of adding mechanism. The advantage in the machine he produced existed in the great increase in rapid manipulation which it offered over the older Art, especially in addition. To improve upon Felt's contribution to the Art of calculating machines from a commercial standpoint demanded a combination that would give still greater possibilities in rapid manipulation.

The patent records show that Felt again came to the front and gave to the public a new machine containing many new combinations of highly-organized mechanism that produced the above-named result. The patents showing these features are Nos. 762,520 and 762,521, the two patents being divisional patents of the same machine.

Felt improvements on Comptometer

Although there were several patents on key-driven calculators issued to others and a key-driven calculator placed on the market, which was sold to some extent, none of these calculators offered anything that would increase the possibility of more rapid manipulation than was to be had from Felt's old Comptometer.

There is one feature about the machine of these two divisional patents which stands out very prominently to those acquainted with the fine points of the physical laws of mechanics. It is a feature that was not printed into the specifications. It may be found only in the time allowed for the mechanical movements to take place, which shows that theoretical reasoning was the foundation for the distribution of the functions in the machine of these patents into increments of time, and that the arrangement of mechanism was especially designed to carry out this primary theoretical reasoning. While it is obvious that such procedure must accompany successful invention of mechanism, it is seldom that we find such fineness displayed as may be found in the timing of the mechanical functions of the later Comptometer.

Scientific distribution of functions

The force of the above statement may be realized by study of the mechanical motions of the old Comptometer and then trying to improve on them to attain greater speed of operation. Such a possibility would depend on more rapid key-strokes.

According to the physical laws of force and motion, to attain greater speed of action demanded a decrease in resistance. Thus, less key resistance must be attained to increase speed of operation.

Felt probably knew from experience that lighter key action could not be had by juggling with springs or by polished surfaces. He was also aware of the infinitesimal space of time allotted to each function, as the parts of the mechanism flew about in the merry dance they performed in whirling the numeral wheels around while under the manipulation of an expert operator. He couldn't see the parts work—he could only theorize when there was trouble; thus he alone knew the difficulties to be met in attempting to make a more rapid calculator.

To describe the mechanism of the new machine from drawings of these patents would leave the reader still in the dark. What was really accomplished can best be understood by reference to the mechanical action in the old Comptometer.

In order that the reader may understand the significance of what was accomplished, let him consider this fact; that the key action of the old "Comptometer" measured as high as eighty-six ounces to a key depression, while in the new machine made under the two named later patents the key depression was reduced to but twenty-two ounces maximum, or a little over a fourth of the power required to operate the keys of the old "Comptometer."

Facts show that a very large part of the resistance met with in the key depression of the old machine was caused by the high tension of the springs which performed the carrying. This high tension was necessary on account of the extremely small fraction of a second allowed for the performance of their function of supplying the power that turned the higher wheel in carrying.

Power consumed by old carrying method

By referring to the description of the inoperative features of the Hill machine (page 25) a parallel example of the time for the carry of the tens in the old Comptometer may be found, showing that but a 1/165 of a second was the allowance.

The carrying means employed in the old Comptometer consisted of levers with dogs or pawls hinged on their free ends, which co-acted with the ten pins of the higher numeral wheels to ratchet them forward a step at a time. The power for supplying such ratcheting action, in the delivery of a carry, was produced in a spring attached to the carrying-lever to actuate it.

The means used to produce the power in the carrying-lever actuating springs, or best termed

Cam and lever carrying mechanism

carrying springs, was through the turning of an envolute cam attached to the lower order numeral wheels, which, acting upon an arm of the carrying levers, forced them away from the wheels, and thus tensioned the carrying springs. The cam and lever is best shown in Fig. 7, page 130.

The timing of the delivery of the carry, as the numeral wheel passed from nine to zero, was brought about by the high point of the cam passing from under the arm of the carrying lever, which, when released, allowed the carrying springs to act and ratchet the higher wheel forward a tenth of a revolution.

This form of carrying action had a peculiarity of reaching a certain set tension when three wheels were employed, so that for all the wheels employed in greater numbers no higher tension was required and no lower tension could be attained. Another feature about this type of transfer device was the fact that to get the set tension as low as possible required that at least eight-tenths of the rotation of the lower wheel should be utilized in camming back the carrying lever or storing the power for the carry. A decrease in this timing meant an increase in the resistance offered in turning the lower wheel by the steeper incline of the cam, and when the wheel in turn received a carry, the increase of resistance increased the work of carrying, and so on by a geometric ratio.

In a recent patent suit, a physical test was made as high as three orders with a one-point cam; that is, a cam operating to store power during a one-tenth rotation of the lower wheel (not an uncommon combination as shown in patents that have been issued), and it was found that by the time the third carrying was reached the springs were so large and powerful that to turn the next wheel would require a railway-coach spring, and that under the same ratio a fifty-four ton hydraulic press would be required to depress the keys in the eighth order.

One-point carrying cam impossible

The foregoing illustration of the idiosyncrasies of mechanical construction offer a good example of why perpetual motion is not possible, viz., that no mechanism was ever made that would not consume a certain per cent of the power delivered to it, through friction and inertia. Of course, expert knowledge of the physical laws of mechanics allow of the application of force along the lines of least resistance, and it is with this feature that the new improvements in the Comptometer have to do.

It would seem that the old carrying means could not be improved upon under the circumstances, but Felt conceived a means which gave more time for the storage of power for the carry and all kinds of time for its delivery, which decreased the power required for carrying by a very large per cent. The means he devised was a motor-type of carrying mechanism that could receive and deliver power at the same time without interference. Thus the full revolution of the lower wheel could be utilized in storage and the same amount of time could be consumed in delivery if necessary, but it was never required.

Felt's improved method of carrying

This tremendous reduction in power required to turn the higher wheel in a carrying operation so decreased the resistance of turning the numeral wheels that the former means used to control the wheels during actuation was unsafe; that is, the old method of jabbing the stop-detent between the pins of the numeral wheel to stop it was not dependable with the increased speed that the numeral wheels revolved, under the reduced resistance.

Again, the feature of time was at issue. The wheels could be whirled at tremendous speed or at a very slow speed. A sudden jab at a key with the finger sent the numeral wheels kiting ahead of the rest of the mechanism so that the detent could not be depended upon to enter between the right pins, which would result in erroneous calculation.

In the new machine, we find that to overcome this unevenness of action, Felt reversed the ratchet action of the denomination actuators, so that no wheel action occurred on their down stroke under the action of the keys, but on the upstroke of the actuators the numeral wheels were turned by the power of the actuator springs stored by the key depression, thus giving an even set rotating action that could not be forced and that could be controlled by a stop detent.

As the timing of this stop-action was coincident with the stopping of the actuators on their upstroke, the actuator was used to perform this function in combination with a detent device that could be released from the wheel independent of the actuators to allow a carry to be delivered.

Gauging and controlling prime actuation

A feature worthy of note connected with this change is displayed in the method in which Felt overcame the timing of the stop action of the actuators in the downward action they received from the keys, which would have been as hard to control as it was to control the wheels under direct key action.

The scheme he devised gave more than double the time to perform the function of intercepting the lightning action with which the actuators moved under a quick key-stroke. The scheme shows a dual alternating stop-action constructed by the use of two stops acting at different levels and co-acting alternately with five equi-spaced stop-shoulders on the front end of the actuators, which were also arranged in different levels.

Alternating stop scheme

The two stops were actuated by the keys in a similar manner to the single stop which co-operated with the pins of the wheel in the old "Comptometer," except that the odd keys operated one stop while the even keys operated the other.

Thus in the new "Comptometer" the (1) key acted to throw the higher level stop into the path of the lowest stop-shoulder on the actuator, and the (2) key acted to throw the lower level stop into the path of the same stop-shoulder on the actuator. In the same manner the (3) and (4) keys caused the odd and even stops to engage the next higher stop-shoulder on the actuator and so on with the rest of the keys.

As the spacing was doubled by the use of but five stop-shoulders, the stops were allowed double the time for entry between the stop-shoulders plus the space that the pin occupied as compared with former method, which was considerably more than double the time allowed for the same function in the old machine.

Besides the redistribution of mechanical functions, another very noteworthy feature is found in these patents which, in the specific means disclosed, constituted another distribution of time for mechanical action. This in the capacity of the machine was what has become commercially known as the "Duplex" feature.

In the old "Comptometer" it was necessary to operate the keys alternately, as a carry from one order to a higher order might be taking place and

Multiplex key action

thus be lost in the action of the higher order wheel while rotating under key-action.

In the machine of the later patents the carry was delayed while the higher-order wheel was under key-action. The construction shown consisted of a latch operated by the actuators, which, when the actuator was depressed, latched up the delivery end of the motor carrying-device so that a carry due to take place at that time would be intercepted until the actuator returned to normal again, at which time the carrying motor device was again free to deliver the carry. This feature allowed the striking of keys in several or all the orders simultaneously, alternately, or any way the operator pleased, which was a great improvement in speedy operativeness.

Control of the carry by the next higher actuator

While the genus of this elastic keyboard invention consisted of control of the carry by the next higher actuator, the specie of the generic feature shown was the delayed control. The first production of this generic feature of control of the carry by the next higher actuator that gave the elastic keyboard-action is shown in the two Felt patents.

It may be argued that this new keyboard feature was simultaneity of key-action and that simultaneity of keyboard-action was old. True it was old, but the flexible simultaneity was new and depended upon individuality of ordinal control for its creation, and Felt created the ordinal control that gave the flexible keyboard.

Simultaneity of key-action was old in key-driven cash registers; such invention as had been disclosed in this line, however, would defeat the usefulness of simultaneity in a key-driven calculator. The useful feature of depressing keys in several orders at once in a key-driven calculating machine lay only in the increased speed of manipulation that it could offer.

Now such simultaneous key-action as had been invented and used on cash registers was not designed with the thought of increasing the speed of manipulation in such machines. The simultaneity of the cash register was designed to compel the operator to depress the keys, which represented the amount of the purchase, exactly simultaneous; otherwise, by manipulation the proper registration could be made to show on the sight-register and a short amount on the total-register. It was a device to keep the clerk or salesman straight and prevent dishonesty.

Forced simultaneous key-action old

If you have ever watched an expert operator using a "Comptometer," try to imagine that operator hesitating to select a group of keys and depressing them exactly simultaneously as one is compelled to do on one of the key-driven cash registers. And then, on the other hand, if you have ever seen a key-driven cash register operated, try to imagine its being operated at the lightning speed at which the "Comptometer" is operated.*

Forced simultaneity applied to a calculator impossible

It must be understood that the exact or forced simultaneity of the cash register scheme, if applied to a calculating machine, would lock the whole keyboard if one of any of a group of keys the operator wished to strike was depressed ahead of the others, and would thus prevent the rest of the group from being depressed until the return of the first key.

---

* In making this comparison, the reader should be careful not to confuse the later key-set crank-driven type like that of Pottin described in the preceding chapter. It was the old key-driven type of cash register which contained the forced simultaneity of key-action.

Flexible simultaneity of key-action a Felt invention

It is within reason that a locking action of that character would even defeat the speed of key-action that was possible on the old "Comptometer," since an operator could overlap the key strokes in that machine to a certain extent; whereas the forced simultaneity of the cash register, if applied to the "Comptometer," would prevent any overlapping or the depression of a second key until the first depressed key returned.

The only simultaneity of key-action that could provide a means of speeding up the old "Comptometer," or any machine of its type, was a means that would leave key-depression free as to matter of time; one that would be perfectly flexible in group manipulation, offering a complete fluidity of motion such as not to hinder the fingering of the operator.

The purpose of the mechanical means employed to give simultaneity in the cash register was to lock all the keys depressed together and lock all others against depression until the former returned. The purpose of mechanical means employed in the Felt patent was to give perfect freedom of key-action, whereas formerly the key manipulation of the old "Comptometer" was restricted in the freedom of key-action, to the extent of being limited to seriatum action.

The above discussion has been somewhat elaborately detailed to offset statements that simultaneity was old in the key-driven Art. There is no question as to the cash-register type of inflexible simultaneity of action being old before Felt patented his flexible type of simultaneity of key-action for a key-driven calculating machine; but any statement intended to convey the idea that Felt's contribution of the flexible simultaneity of key-action to the Art was not new, must come from ignorance of the facts or malice aforethought.

This flexible keyboard "Comptometer" was given the trade-name of "Duplex Comptometer;" the term "Duplex" meaning that two keys could be depressed, as distinguished from the seriatum one at a time key-action formerly required. The term, however, fell short of setting forth the capacity of such action, as it was, in fact, not restricted to mere duplex-action—it was really a multiplex key-action having no limit except the lack of fingers on the part of the operator to depress the keys.

Duplex Comptometer

The validity of these patents has been sustained in litigation. The technical scope of the mere claims has been disputed, as patent claims sometimes are; but the broad newness and importance of the practical calculative capacity achieved is beyond dispute. The recent machine called the "Burroughs Calculator" has multiplex key-action, but it did nothing to advance the practical capacity of key-driven calculating machines.

The operation of key-driven machines has always been attended more or less with a feeling that a key-stroke may not have been completed, especially by a novice in operating. Recognition of the possibility of errors occurring through incomplete key-strokes in key-driven adding mechanism was first disclosed as early as 1872 in the Robjohn patent (see page 36), in which a full-stroke device is shown co-acting with the keys.

Introduction of full-stroke mechanism

In the drawings it will be noted that for each key there is provided a ratchet device co-operating with the key to compel a full-stroke. This scheme, like other similar later attempts, was aimed at the prevention of an error in the operation of adding mechanism, but as a means of prevention of an error it was lacking, because unless the operator noticed that the key had not returned the next key depressed would, through the action of the rotor, pull the partly depressed key way down until it was released, when it would rise again, possibly without the knowledge of the operator. There still remained the fact that the occurrence of the error was not made known to the operator until it was too late to correct it.

Error signal keyboard

That Felt was interested in the solution of the problem for detection and correction of the errors in key-strokes is shown in the several patents issued to him on features pertaining to this subject. After numerous experiments Felt came to the conclusion that it was futile to lock a key in event of a partial stroke and that the solution lay in the locking of the keys in the other orders from that in which the error had been made, thus signaling the operator and compelling correction before further manipulation could be accomplished.

Again we find, as with the simultaneity of key-action, that a question may be raised as to the novelty of invention by those who wish to say that there are full-stroke mechanisms in the key-driven cash register Art that lock the rest of the keyboard. But the key-locks disclosed in the cash register were directed to a continuity of stroke engroup, as distinguished from the individualism necessary to the key-driven calculator.

The mechanical means employed, of course, varied greatly from that which would be of any value in the calculating machine Art, and the theoretical scheme was aimed at a widely different result. Flexibility was necessary.

The feature sought by Felt for his calculator was a signal to the operator that an error had been made—if an error should occur—and to block the operation of any of the other orders until the error was corrected. This he accomplished by causing all the other orders to be locked against manipulation, through the occurrence of an error in a key-stroke; thus preventing manipulation of another order until the error was corrected.

Locking of the other orders by a short key-stroke

Now it may be said that the locking of other orders was old in the cash register; but let us analyze the scheme and action of both. The depression of a key of the key-driven cash register immediately locked all other keys not depressed, and retained such locking-action during depression and until the complete return of such key-depression; thus the keyboard was locked, error or no error.

Inactive keys locked during proper key-action in cash register

A correct depression of a key in Felt's new invention, as applied to key-driven calculators, does not lock the rest of the keys. In fact, no key of Felt's invention is locked until an error occurs.

Inactive keys not locked during proper key-action in "Comptometer"

The lock of the key-driven cash register is a lock that takes effect without an error having occurred—one that is always present with respect to the keys not depressed simultaneously, and a feature designed to force simultaneity of group key-action to prevent, as before explained, dishonesty.

The lock of the key-driven calculator inventions referred to are in no way connected with simultaneous key-action—as in the cash register—and never act to lock the other orders except when there is an error in a key-stroke. As the writer has explained respecting the simultaneous feature of the cash register, the locking of the other orders in the cash register interfered with the flexibility of the key-action and for that reason would be impossible in a key-driven calculator, where rapid manipulation is dependent on flexibility.

The scheme of the new key-driven calculator inventions referred to, were designed to allow perfect freedom of individual key-action and to block such action only when an error in any individual key-stroke should be made. There is nothing in common in the two schemes. The time, purpose and mechanical means employed differ entirely.

"Controlled-key Comptometer"

This new idea of Felt's is embodied in what is commercially known as the "Controlled-key Duplex Comptometer." The term "Controlled-key" was coined to fit this broadly new combination, but a word coined to fit the functions of a new mechanism is seldom enough to convey a complete understanding of its true qualities.

Aside from the broad newness of the Felt "Controlled-key" feature referred to, even the mechanical means for safeguarding the individual key-action was new in its application as a full-stroke device. The means employed operated directly on the accumulator mechanism, locking it against registration until the error was corrected, which differed greatly from the devices applied to the keys or actuators designed by others to bring about a similar result. But the locking of all the other orders of mechanism, through any key-action short of a full stroke, as a signal or error, has no mechanical equivalent or simile in the Art.

The Improved Recorder

SINCE the general installation of the recording-adder by the banks, the minds of "get-rich-quick" inventors have been turned toward this type of machine. The result has been that a vast number of patents on such machines were issued, a large proportion of which represent worthless and impossible mechanism purported by their inventors to contain improvements on the Art. Some of these patents on alleged improvements describe and purport to contain features, that, if really made operative in an operative machine, would be useful to the public. But as inventions, they merely illustrate the conceptions of a new and useful feature that can never be of use to anyone until put into concrete operative form.

The mass of recorder inventions patented

To describe these features would be useless, as they have not advanced the Art; they merely act to retard its advancement through the patent rights that are granted on the hatched-up inoperative devices or mechanism purported to hold such features.

Of the vast number of patents issued, but few of the machines represented therein have ever reached the market, and of these machines, except those previously mentioned, there is little that may be said respecting new elementary features that may be called an advancement of the Art. It is to be expected, of course, that the manufacturer of such machines will not hold the same opinion as the writer on this subject. But the fact that the

But few of the recorder patents of value

generic principles of recording the items and totals were worked out before they even thought of constructing such a machine leaves little chance for anything but specific features of construction for them to make that may be considered new.

Reserve inven-
tion as good
insurance

Another feature to be considered in this line is that while these new manufacturers were working out the "kinks" or fine adjustments, which can only be determined after a considerable number of machines have been put into service, the older manufacturers were working or had worked out and held in reserve new improvements that were not obvious to those new at the game.

It is quite common for manufacturers to have a reserved stock of improved features to draw from. In fact, such a stock is sometimes the best insurance they have against being run out of business by a competitor who places a machine on the market to undersell them. Of course, all manufacturers believe they purvey the best and advise the public relative to this point in their advertisements.

Erroneous
advertising

One manufacturer of a recording-adder, a much later invention than either the Felt or Burroughs recorder, circulated some advertising pamphlets once which contained a statement that their machine was the first visible recorder. A reproduction of this pamphlet is shown on the opposite page. The reader will at once recognize the error in such a statement, as the first Felt recorder was a visible printer.

The statement seems extremely peculiar after paying tribute to Felt as the pioneer in the Art of adding machines. One would suppose that having knowledge enough of the Art to offer such trib-

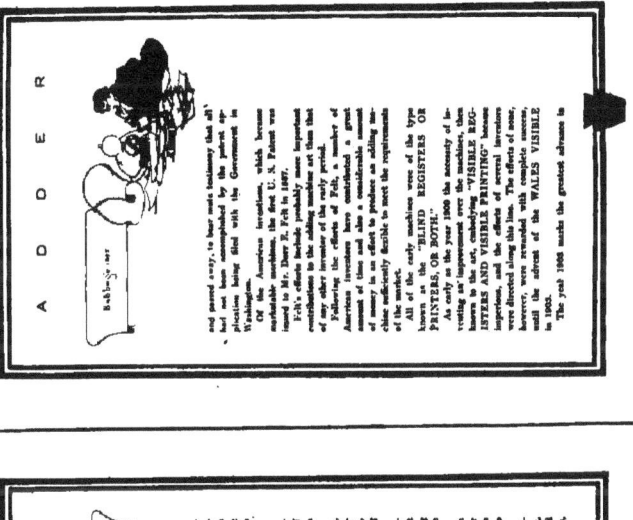

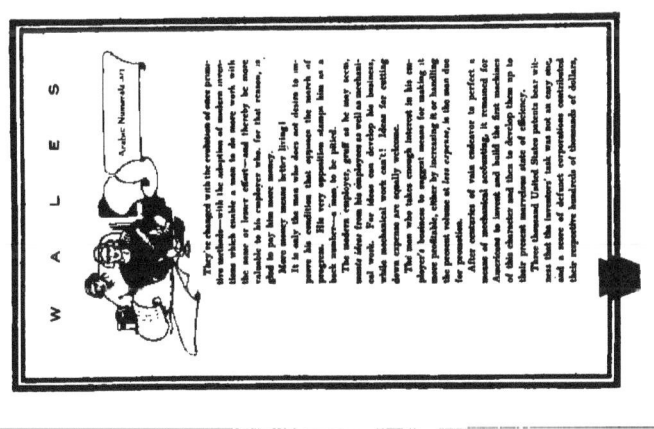

Two Pages from Booklet Issued by
Wales Adding Machine Co.

ute would have left them better advised on the subject of visible recording.

Error key The first of the later improvements in the key-set crank-operated recorder were made by Burroughs and consisted of the features which formed a part of Burroughs patent No. 504,963 of 1893. One of these features consisted of means provided in the shape of a special key that when depressed would clear the key-setting, thus allowing of an erroneous key-setting to be corrected by clearing and resetting the correct item.

Sub-total Another feature was provision for printing a total at any time without clearing the machine, thus allowing printing of what may be called a sub-total, while the grand total is carried on to be printed later.

Repeat key The third feature consisted of means for repeated addition and recording of the same item. The means provided consisted of a key, which, if depressed after setting an item on the keys, would prevent the keys from being cleared; thus by repeated operation of the hand-crank the item set up would be printed and added repeatedly.

Locked keyboard The next feature was one of construction, as it was designed to overcome the possibility of the setting of two keys in the same order, by locking all the other keys in that order. The invention was shown applied to the Burroughs machine, but was applied for by Wm. H. Pike, Jr., and was issued January 13, 1898.

Quick paper return In 1900 Felt perfected a quick paper return for his wide paper-carriage and applied for a patent, which was issued March 11, 1902, the number of which is 694,955. The feature was, that by operating a lever, it served to return the paper after recording a column of items and automatically shifted the carriage ready for the recording of another column of items, thus facilitating speedy operation.

Paper stop — In March, 1902, a patent was allowed Felt on means to lock the mechanism in a recorder when the paper was about to run out of the rolls; a feature which, in tabulating, served as a check against the paper running out of the rolls and prevented further operation until the paper was shifted to commence a new column of items, thus insuring the printing of each record on the paper which formerly depended upon the vigilance of the operator.

Cross tabulating — The next feature in the recording machine Art which shows a new operative feature, that may be considered an improvement, is cross-tabulating. It consisted of means for horizontal tabulating or recording across a sheet of paper as well as in vertical columns. While this feature was for special use, it served to broaden the usefulness of the recorder in bringing together classified balances by dates with cross-added totals, and many other similar uses. This feature was the invention of D. E. Felt, who applied for a patent April 29, 1901, which was issued October 21, 1902; the patent number is 711,407.

Item stop — Another special feature serving to broaden the usefulness of the recording-adder was invented by Felt, and may be found in patent No. 780,272, applied for March 30, 1901, and issued January 17, 1905. This feature was a device which controlled the printing of a predetermined number of items which could be set by the operator, and which, when the predetermined number had been printed, would lock the mechanism against further action until the paper was shifted to print a new column.

Motor drive

Prior to May 9, 1901, there is no record of any recording-adder having been operated by electric motor drive. But on that date Frank C. Rinche applied for a patent showing such a combination with the recorder, which became commercially known as the Universal Accountant. The patent, No. 726,803, was issued April 28, 1903, and is the first of a series issued to Rinche on various combinations of mechanical driving connections.

Distinguishing marks for clear, totals and sub-totals

A feature common to recording of added columns of numerical items is the distinguishing characters for clear, sub-totals and totals by the use of letters, stars and other marks. The first patent on anything of this nature that has come into general use was applied for June 9, 1903, by A. Macauley, and was issued June 12, 1906. This patent is No. 823,474, and shown connected with the Burroughs recorder to register with a star when the first item is printed if the machine is clear and when a total is printing. Provision was also made for printing an S when a sub-total was printed.

Adding cut-out

The use of recording-adders is often applied when it is desired to record dates along with tabulating added columns of recorded items. Of course there is no use of adding the dates together, and again if they were allowed to be added to the totals an erroneous total of the columns added may result under certain conditions. Means for automatically cutting out additions at certain positions of the paper carriage in cross-line tabulating was devised by H. C. Peters, and a patent showing such combination operative on the Burroughs recorder was applied for by him May 12, 1904. The patent, No. 1,028,133, was issued June 4, 1912.

With the introduction of the key-set crank-operated feature on the Felt Comptometer, the key action, like in the Burroughs recorder, became a feature to be considered; but unlike the organism of the Burroughs, the Felt construction allowed of the use of a self-correcting keyboard without the possibility of error occurring from its use. This feature is shown in a patent issued to Felt & Wetmore applied for December 27, 1904, and issued May 14, 1907. The patent number is 853,543, and provides a means of correcting errors made in setting the keys by merely depressing the proper key or keys, which will release any previously set in the respective orders. *Self-correcting keyboard*

In some classes of recording it is desirable to print more than one column of items without shifting the paper carriage laterally. A means providing for such an emergency is shown in patent No. 825,205, issued to C. W. Gooch July 3, 1906. The patent was applied for December 2, 1905, and shows a means applicable to any order that may intercept the printing of the ciphers in that order, and thereby the ciphers in all other orders to the right from any key depression to the left of such order. This made what has been generally known as the split keyboard, but differs from that now in general use in that it was set to certain orders and not selective at the will of the operator. *Split keyboard*

With the coming of the motor-operated recording-adders, the extra time allowed the operator, through being relieved of having to work the crank back and forth, left a lapse of time until the motor finished its cranking of the machine. In other words, there could be no gain in the speed of operation because it took as much time for the *Dual action keyboard* motor to operate the machine as it did by human power. In a patent granted to McFarland, No. 895,664, applied for October 19, 1905, is shown a means for utilizing the lapse of time which the operator was formerly obliged to lose while waiting for the motor to finish its operation of cranking the machine. It is shown in combination with the keyboard of the Pike recorder and consists of a change that allows the keys for the next item to be set while the motor is cranking the machine to print and add the item previously set, thus utilizing the time formerly lost.

Non-add signal

In adding and recording columns of figures, it quite often happens that it is desirable to print a number without adding it into the total, which may be accomplished in general by depressing the non-add key or knob, or what may be supplied for that purpose. These numbers, however, were not provided with any means by which they could be distinguished from those added into the total until Jesse G. Vincent conceived the idea of printing a distinguishing mark beside them to designate that they were mere numbers not added to the total. The means for accomplishing this feature is shown in patent No. 1,043,883, applied for September 24, 1906, and issued November 12, 1912.

Selective split keyboard

A new improvement in the split keyboard formerly devised by C. W. Gooch is shown in a patent issued to Wetmore & Niemann applied to the Felt "Comptograph." This improvement consists of a selective device for splitting the keyboard into four different combinations selective to any combination. The patent was applied for April 24, 1907, and issued February 2, 1915; the number is 1,127,332.

In some classes of recording it is desirable at times to cut out the printing of some of the orders and in others the whole of the printing mechanism. Mr. Fred A. Niemann patented a means for such a contingency. The patent was applied for April 24, 1907, but was not issued until March 9, 1920. The feature was shown applied to the Felt Comptograph for tabulating or printing vertically a series of added and footed columns of figures.

Selective printing cut-out

It is sometimes desirable to print the sum of all the totals of the footed columns or what may be called a grand total. William E. Swalm, in patent No. 885,202, applied for October 24, 1907, and issued April 21, 1908, shows how this feature may be accomplished on the Burroughs recorder. It consisted of an extra series of accumulator wheels that could be meshed with the regular accumulator wheels, and thus receive actuation resulting in accumulation, the same as the regular wheels. When, however, the regular wheels are zeroized in printing the individual totals, the extra accumulator wheels are left out of mesh. Thus the grand totals are accumulated. The printing of the grand total is accomplished by the meshing of the grand total wheels with the regular and the usual operation of taking a regular total. The regular wheels, however, must be cleared first.

Grand totalizer

The shuttle carriage, a means devised to print two columns of figures by printing a number in one column and a sum in the other by alternate action, was the conception of Clyde E. Gardner, and is shown applied to the carriage of the Pike recorder in patent No. 1,052,811 of February 11, 1913. The patent was applied for September 24, 1908, and consists of means for automatically shifting the carriage back and forth.

Alternate cross printing

Determinate item signal

Another means than that invented by Felt to signal the operator when a predetermined number of items have been recorded, consists of a bell, which rings to notify the operator to that effect. This signal was the invention of J. G. Vincent, and is shown in patent No. 968,005 of August 23, 1910, and was applied for December 3, 1909, as an attachment to the carriage of the Burroughs machine.

Subtraction by reverse action

Although subtraction has always been accomplished on this type of machine as a means of correcting an error, it was always accomplished on the Burroughs recorder by the use of what is generally known as the complimental method, which, without special provision, is rather objectionable. On the 22d of April, 1910, Wm. E. Swalm applied for a patent which was issued June 4, which shows means connected with the Burroughs machine that allowed subtraction to be made by the direct method by setting the keys the same as for addition. The patent number is 1,028,149.

Selective split for keyboard

A further improvement on the split keyboard feature is shown in a patent issued to Fred A. Niemann in which is shown an individually selective cipher cut-out that splits the keyboard into any combination at the will of the operator. The said patent is No. 1,309,692, applied for October 7, 1912, and issued July 15, 1919, and shows the improvement in combination with the Felt "Comptograph."

Rapid paper insert and ejector

In some classes of listing or tabulating it is an advantage to enter the paper and eject it with a rapidity that will facilitate the handling of a large number of sheets, such for instance as the usual bank statements. In patent No. 1,208,375

F. C. Rinche shows how he accomplished this feature on the Burroughs recorder. The patent was applied for July 21, 1913, and issued December 12, 1916.

Of the named improvements, of course, all are designed to fit the requirements of the machines they are shown as a part of in the drawings of the patent. They are also claimed as adaptable to other machines of the type, but some are so specific to the machine they form an improvement on that they are not adaptable to other makes. Again some give results on the machine they form a part of that was accomplished in a different way in another make.

Most of the improvements named, however, are of such a nature that the broad feature disclosed is adaptable to all makes if mechanism should be specially designed to suit such machines that will function to give the result.

The Bookkeeping and Billing Machine

AN outgrowth of the recording-machine Art is represented in a new type of recording machine especially adapted to bookkeeping and the making out of invoices or reports where typewriting combined with arithmetical recording is necessary. This class of work demands a combination of the typewriter with adding and multiplying mechanism, having a capacity for printing the totals of either addition or multiplication.

Early Combinations

Several attempts have been made to combine the typewriter and adding-recorder; and there have been combinations of multiplying and recording. Another combination that has been used to some extent for bookkeeping and billing is an adding attachment for typewriters, but all these combinations were lacking in one feature or another of what may be called a real bookkeeping machine and billing machine.

The combination of the typewriter and multiple-order keyboard recording-adders was too cumbersome, and the means employed for multiplication on such machines required too many manipulative motions from the operator. In simple cases of multiplication as high as fifty manipulative motions would be required to perform an example on such a machine.

The combination of multiplying mechanism, either direct or by repeated stroke, with the

"Moon-Hopkins" Billing and Bookkeeping Machine

multiple keyboard has been made, but without the typewriting feature they do not serve as a real bookkeeping and billing machine.

The combination of the typewriter and the adding attachment lacks automatic means to print totals. The operator must read the totals and print them with the typewriter. Multiplication on such a combination is, of course, out of the question.

The culmination of the quest for a practical bookkeeping machine is a peculiar one, as it was dependent upon the ten-key recorder, which has never become as popular as the multiple-order keyboard on account of its limited capacity. The simplicity of its keyboard, however, lent to its combination with the typewriter, and the application of direct multiplication removed a large per cent of the limitation which formerly stood as an objection to this class of machine when multiplication becomes necessary.

First Practical Combination

For the combination, which finally produced the desired result, we must thank Mr. Hubert Hopkins, who is not only the patentee of such a combination, but also the inventor of the first practical ten-key recording-adder which has become commercially known as the "Dalton" machine.

His bookkeeping machine is commercially known as the "Moon-Hopkins Billing Machine." See illustration on opposite page.

Moon-Hopkins Billing Machine

The term "Bookkeeping Machine" has been misused by applying it to machines which only perform some of the functions of bookkeeping.

It is unnecessary to go into the history of the Hopkins Bookkeeping Machine to show the evolution of the Art relative to this class of machines, as the features that have made such a machine practical were developed by Hopkins himself, and

The principle of "Napier's Bones" may be easily explained by imagining ten rectangular slips of cardboard, each divided into nine squares. In the top squares of the slips the ten digits are written, and each slip contains in its nine squares the first nine multiples of the digit which appears in the top square. With the exception of the top square, every square is divided into parts by a diagonal, the units being written on one side and the tens on the other, so that when a multiple consists of two figures they are separated by the diagonal. Fig. 1 shows the slips corresponding to the numbers 2, 0, 8, 5, placed side by side in contact with one another, and next to them is placed another slip containing, in squares without diagonals, the first nine digits. The slips thus placed in contact give the multiples of the number 2085, the digits in each parallelogram being added together; for example, corresponding to the number 6 on the right-hand slip we have 0, 8+3, 0+4, 2, 1, whence we find 0, 1, 5, 2, 1 as the digits, written backwards, of 6×2085. The use of the slips for the purpose of multiplication is now evident, thus, to multiply 2085 by 736 we take out in this manner the multiples corresponding to 6, 3, 7 and set down the digits as they are obtained, from right to left, shifting them back one place and adding up the columns as in ordinary multiplication, viz., the figures as written down are

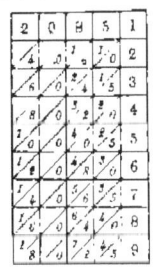

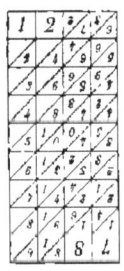

$$\begin{array}{r}12510\\6255\\14595\\\hline 1534560\end{array}$$

Napier's rods or bones consist of ten oblong pieces of wood or other material with square ends. Each of the four faces of each rod contains multiples of one of the nine digits, and is similar to one of the slips just described, the first rod containing the multiples of 0, 1, 9, 8, the second of 0, 2, 9, 7, the third of 0, 3, 9, 6, the fourth of 0, 4, 9, 5, the fifth of 1, 2, 8, 7, the sixth of 1, 3, 8, 6, the seventh of 1, 4, 8, 5, the eighth of 2, 3, 7, 6, the ninth of 2, 4, 7, 5, and the tenth of 3, 4, 6, 5. Each rod, therefore, contains

FIG. 1.   FIG. 2.

on two of its faces multiples of digits which are complementary to those on the other two faces; and the multiples of a digit and its complement are reversed in position. The arrangements of the numbers on the rods will be evident from fig. 2, which represents the four faces of the fifth bar. The set of ten rods is thus equivalent to four sets of slips as described above.

Napier's Bones
From Napier Tercentenary Celebration Handbook

From Drawings of Barbour Patent No. 130,404

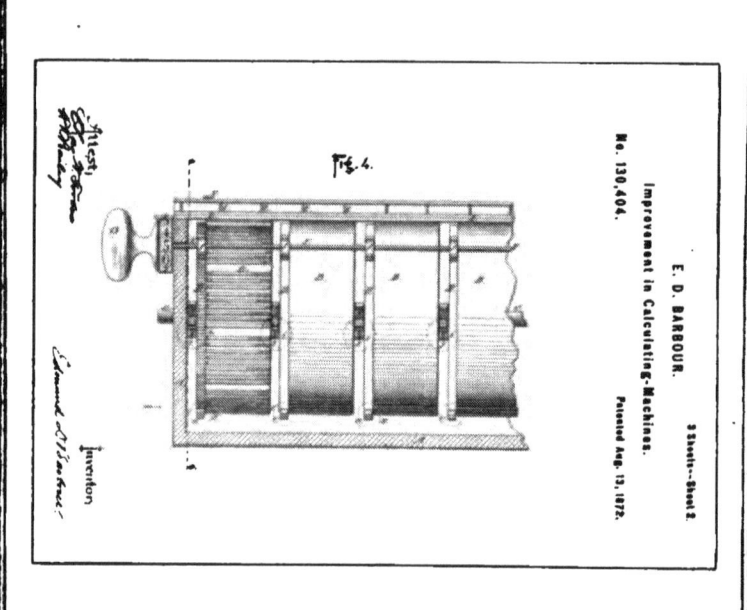

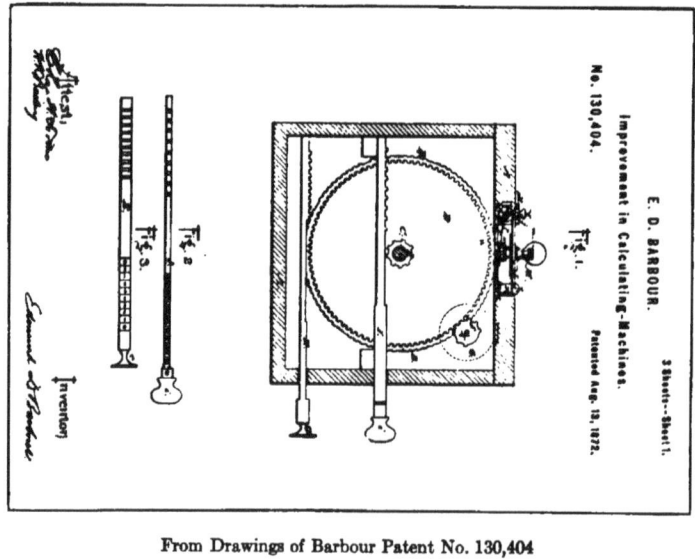

at the present date there is none to dispute the title since his is the only machine having the required combination referred to. The scheme used by Hopkins for multiplication in his billing machine is, as stated, direct multiplication or that of adding the multiples of digits directly to the accumulator numeral wheels instead of pumping it into the accumulator wheels by repeated addition of the digits as is more commonly used.

The direct method of multiplying is old, as a matter of fact, the first mechanical means employed for multiplying worked by the direct method. But its combination with recording and typewriter mechanism invented by Hopkins was new.

Napier, in 1620, laid the foundation of the mechanical method of direct multiplication when he invented his multiplying bones. The scheme of overlapping the ordinal places is shown in the diagonal lines used to separate units from the tens in each multiple of the nine digits (see illustration, page 179), thus providing a convenient means by which the ordinal values may be added together.

Napier's bones first direct multiplier

The first attempt to set Napier's scheme to mechanism that would add and register the overlapping ordinal values was patented by E. D. Barbour in 1872. See reproduction of patent drawings on opposite page.

First direct multiplying machine

THE BARBOUR MULTIPLIER

The accumulator mechanism of the Barbour machine, including the numeral wheels and their devices for transferring the tens, is mounted in a sliding carriage at the top of the machine (see Fig. 1), which may be operated by the hand-knob.

Extending through the bottom of the carriage are a series of pinions, one for each ordinal nu-

John Napier

Description of Barbour Multiplier

meral wheel, and connected thereto by a ratchet and pawl action. The pinions are each so arranged as to be operative with a gear rack beneath the carriage when the carriage is slid back and forth.

Thus the wheels received action from one direction of the motion of the carriage and remain idle during the movement in the other direction. The degree of motion so received would, of course, depend upon the number of teeth in the racks below encountered by the pinions.

The gear racks employed by Barbour were numerous, one being provided for each multiple of the nine digits, arranged in groups constituting nine sets mounted on the drums marked B (see Fig. 4). Each of these sets contain nine mutilated gear racks, the arrangement of the teeth of which serve as the multiples of the digit they represent.

The teeth of the racks representing the multiples of the digits were arranged in groups of units and tens. For instance: 4×6=24, the rack representing the multiple of 4×6 would have two gear teeth in the tens place and four gear teeth in the units place, and likewise for the eighty other combinations.

Adding the multiples of the digits by overlapping the orders was accomplished by a very simple means, the arrangement of the racks being such that as the carriage was moved from left to right the numeral wheel pinions would move over the units rack teeth of a multiplying rack of one order and the tens rack teeth of a multiplying rack in the next lower order.

By close examination the reader will note from the drawings that the lower one of the sets of multiplying gear racks shown on the drum B, to the left in Fig. 4, is the series of one times the nine digits, the next set or series of racks above are the multiplying racks for the multiples of two, the lowest rack in that series having but two teeth, the next higher rack four teeth, the next rack six and the next eight.

So far no multiple of two has amounted to more than a units ordinal place, therefore these racks operate on a lower-order numeral wheel, and are all placed to the right of the center on the drum B, but the next rack above for adding the multiple of two times five requires that one shall be added to a higher order, and is therefore placed on the left side of the center of the drum.

Thus it will be noted that by reading the number of teeth on the right of each rack as units and those on the left as tens, that running anti-clockwise around the drum, each series of multiplying racks show multiples of the digits from one to four, it being obvious that the racks for adding the multiples of the higher digits are on the opposite side of the drums.

From the layout of the racks it is also obvious that the starting or normal position of the carriage would be with the numeral wheel pinions of each order in the center of each drum, so that as the carriage is moved to the right the units wheel will receive movement from the units teeth of the rack on the units drum, while the tens wheel will receive movement from the units teeth of the tens drum and the tens teeth of the units drum, and so on with the higher wheels, as each numeral wheel pinion except the units passes from the center of one drum to the center of the next lower and engages such teeth as may be presented.

Each of the drums B are independently mounted on the pivot shaft C, and are provided with the hand-operating setting-racks I and E, co-acting with the gears R and D, to help in bringing the proper racks into engageable positions with the pinions of the accumulator numeral or total wheels.

The hand-knob G, Fig. 4, and the gears f, fast to a common shaft, furnish a means for operating the whole series of drums when the right multiple series of racks of each drum have been brought into position.

As an example of the operation of the Barbour calculator, let us assume that 7894 is to be multiplied by 348. The first drum to the right would be moved by its setting racks until the series of multiplying racks for adding the multiples of four are presented, the next higher drum to the left would be set until the series of multiplying racks for adding the multiples of nine were presented, the next higher drum would be set for the multiples of eight, and the next higher drum, or the fourth to the left, would be set for the multiples of seven. Then the hand-knob G, first turned to register zero, may be shoved to the right, engaging the pinions f with the gears D, and by turning the knob to register (8), the first figure in the multiplier, the racks are then set ready to move the numeral wheels to register as follows: The drum to the right or the units drum has presented the multiplying rack for adding the multiple of 8×4, thus it will present three teeth for the tens wheel and two teeth for the units wheel. The tens drum presenting the rack for adding the multiple of 8×9 will present seven teeth for the hundreds wheel and two for the tens wheel. The

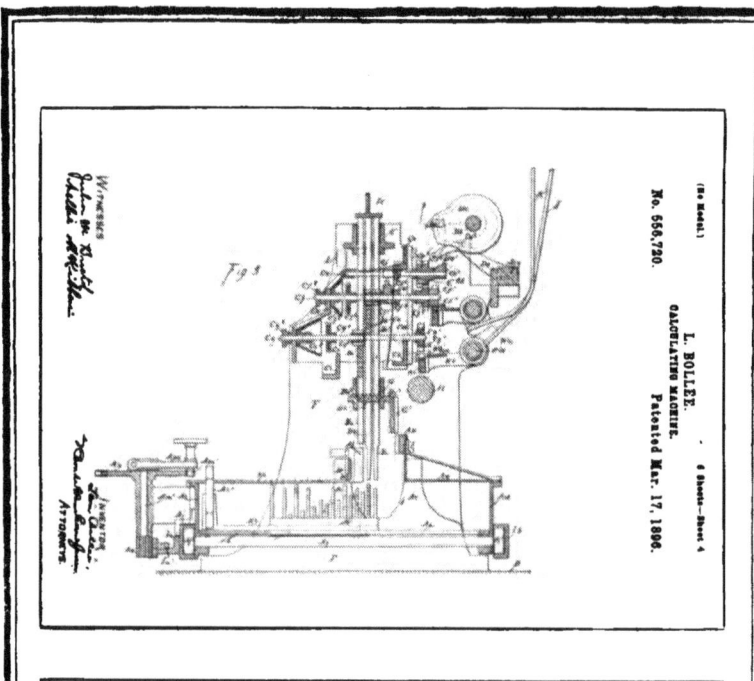

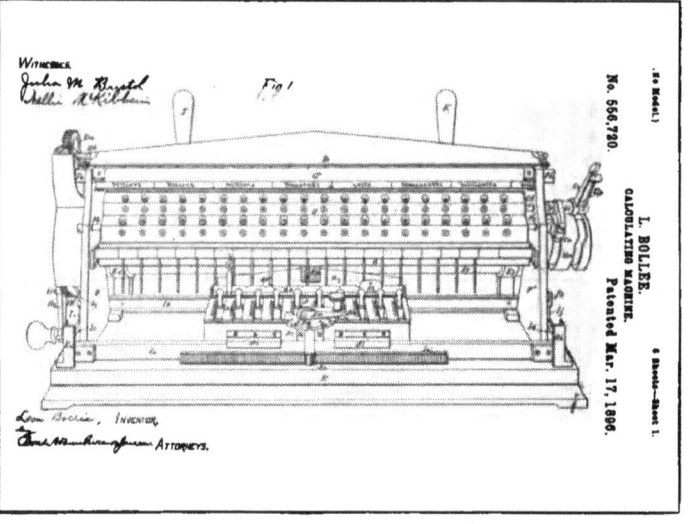

From Drawings of Bollee Patent No. 556,720

hundreds drum presenting the rack for adding the multiple of 8×8 will present six teeth for the thousands wheel and four for the hundreds wheel.

The rack of the thousands drum representing the multiple of 8×7 will present five teeth for the tens of thousands wheel and six for the thousands wheel. Thus by sliding the carriage to the right one space, the numeral wheel pinions will engage first the units teeth on one drum, then the tens teeth on the next lower drum and cause the wheels to register 63152. The operator, by turning the knob G to register (4), the next figure of the multiplier, turns the drum so that a series of multiplying racks representing multiples of 4 times each figure in the multiplicand are presented, so that by sliding the carriage another space to the right, the multiple of 4×7894 will be added to the numeral wheels. The operator then turns the knob to register three and moves the carriage one more space to the right, adding the multiple of 3×7894 to the wheels in the next higher ordinal series, resulting in the answer of 2747112.

There are, of course, many questionable features about the construction shown in the machine of the Barbour patent, but as a feature of historic interest it is worthy of consideration, like many other attempts in the early Art.

The Bollee Multiplier

Probably the first successful direct multiplying machine was made by Leon Bollee, a Frenchman, who patented his invention in France in 1889. A patent on the Bollee machine was applied for in this country and was issued March 17, 1896, some of the drawings of which are reproduced on the opposite page.

Description of Bollee Machine

Instead of using eighty-one multiplying gear racks for each order as in the Barbour patent, Bollee used but two gear racks for each order; one for adding the units and the other for adding the tens; these racks operate vertically and are marked respectively Bb and Bc. (See Fig. 3.)

The racks are frictionally held against gravity in the permanent framework of the machine, and are moved up and down by contact at each end, received from above by bar Ie, and from below by pins of varying length set in the movable plates Ab.

The bar Ie forms part of a reciprocating frame which moves vertically and in which are slidably mounted the pin plates Ab. These plates are what Bollee called his "mechanical multiplication tables."

The arrangement of the pins and their lengths are such as to give degrees of additive movement to the units and tens gear racks equal to the multiplying racks in the Barbour multiplier.

The pin plates are moved by the hand-knobs Ab², and the plate shown in Fig. 3 is positioned for multiples of nine.

The means for setting the multiples correspond to the index hand-knob of the Barbour machine, and consists of the crank Am, which, when operated, shifts the whole series of plates laterally. A graduated dial serves the operator to set the multiple that the multiplicand, set by the positioning of the plates, is to be multiplied by.

The accumulator mechanism is mounted in a reciprocating frame which moves horizontally, causing the gears of the numeral wheels to engage first the units racks on their upstroke under action of the pins, and then the tens racks on their downstroke under the action of the top bar of the vertically moving frame, the downward motion, of course, being regulated by the upward movement it receives from the pin that forces it up.

As may be noted in Fig. 1, the multiplying plates are held in a laterally movable carriage that is shifted through the turning of the multiplier factor setting hand crank Am, by means of the rack and pinion action. This gearing is such that each revolution moves the multiplying plates under a higher or lower series of orders, thus allowing the multiples of a higher or lower order series to be added in the process of multiplication or subtracted in division, as the case may be.

Although the Bollee machine is reputed to be a practical machine, as is attested from the models on exhibit in the Museum of Des Arts and Metiers of Paris in France, it was never manufactured and placed on the market.

Bollee's principle has, however, been commercialized by a Swiss manufacturer in a machine made and sold under the trade-name of "The Millionaire," the U. S. patents of which were applied for and issued to Steiger.

Bollee's principle commercialized.

Hopkins constructed his multiplying mechanism on the Bollee scheme of using stepped controlling plates for his reciprocating racks to give the multiples of the digits, but the ingenious method of application shown in the Hopkins patent drawings illustrates well the American foresight of simplicity of manufacture.

During the past ten years there have been a large number of patents applied for on mechanism containing the same general scheme as that of Bollee and Steiger, but up to the present writing no machines with direct multiplying mechanism have been commercialized except "The Millionaire," which is non-recording, and "Moon-Hopkins Bookkeeping Machine."

A Closing Word

AS previously stated, it is impossible to describe or illustrate the thousands of inventions that have been patented in the Art of accounting machines, and some of the inventors may feel that the writer has shown partiality. The subject of this book, however, has to do only with the Art as it stands commercialized and those who are responsible for its existence.

In the arguments to prove validity of contributions of vital importance to the Art, many other patented machines have been used which really have no bearing on the Art. But the writer was obliged to show their defects, otherwise the misconception derived from articles written by authors incompetent to judge would leave the public in error as to the real truth relative to the Art of the modern accounting machines.

That all inventors deserve credit, even in the face of failure, is without question. The hours, days, months, and sometimes years, given up to the working out of any machine, intended to benefit mankind, whether the result brings a return or not,—whether the invention holds value, or no,—leaves a record that the world may benefit by, in pointing out the errors or productive results.

If it were not for the ambitions and untiring efforts of men of this type, who give heart and soul to the working out of intricate problems, the world would not be as far advanced as it is today.

The writer has kept in close touch with the Art of calculating machines since 1893, and made exhaustive research of it prior to that period. There have been thousands of patents issued on machines of the class herein set forth, but outside of the features reviewed there have been no broadly new ones of practical importance that have as yet proved to be of great value to the public. What is in the making, and what may be developed later, is open to conjecture. It is a safe conjecture, however, that in the present high state of the Art it will tax the wits of high-class engineers to offer any substantial and broadly-new feature which will be heralded as a noticeable step in the Art. And that, as in the past, thousands of mistakes, and impractical as well as inoperative machines will be made and patented, to one that will hold real value.

Index to Subjects

Types of Ancient and Modern Machines   Page
- General knowledge lacking 5
- Key-driven machine, first of the modern machines 6
- Recording, the primary feature of adding machines that print 7
- Validity and priority of invention 8
- Description of Pascal's invention 11
- Constructional features of the Pascal machine 12
- Increased capacity of modern calculator 13
- Patent office a repository of ineffectual efforts 14

The Early Key-Driven Art
- First attempt to use depressable keys for adding was made in America 17
- Description of Parmelee machine 18
- Foreign digit adders 18
- Single-digit adders lack capacity 19
- Some early U. S. patents on single-digit adding machines 20
- Calculating machines in use abroad for centuries 21
- First key-driven machines no improvement to the Art ... 21
- Description of the Hill machine 22
- Hill machine at National Museum 25
- Inoperativeness of Hill machine 25
- High speed of key drive 26
- Camera slow compared with carry of the tens 26
- Hill machine merely adding mechanism, incomplete as operative machine 29
- Chapin and Stark patents 29
- Description of Chapin machine 29
- Inoperativeness of Chapin machine 30
- Description of Stark machine 33
- Inoperativeness of Stark machine 37
- Nine keys common to a plurality of orders 37
- Description of Robjohn machine 38
- First control for a carried numeral wheel 41
- Description of Bouchet machine 42
- Bouchet machine marketed 43
- Misuse of the term "Calculating Machine" 43
- Description of Spaulding machine 47
- Prime actuation of a carried wheel impossible in the Spalding machine 49

The Key-Driven Calculator

	Page
Theory versus the concrete	50
All but one of the generic elements solved	51
Originality of inventions	51
A conception which led to the final solution	52
Evolution of an invention	55
Trials of an inventor	55
The first "Comptometer"	56
Felt patent 371,496	56
Description of Felt calculator	59
Recapitulation of Art prior to Felt calculator	60
Why Hill failed to produce an operative machine	61
Idiosyncrasies of force and motion increased by use of keys	61
Light construction a feature	62
Operative features necessary	62
Classification of the features contained in the early Art of key-driven machines	63
Carrying mechanism of Felt's calculator	63
Transfer devices	64
Carrying mechanism versus mere transfer devices	64
Details of Felt carrying mechanism	65
Manufacture of the Felt calculator	69
Trade name of Felt calculator	70
Felt calculator exhibit at National Museum	70
Significant proof of Felt's claim of priority	75
Rules for operation an important factor of modern calculator	76

Early Efforts in the Recording Machine Art

First attempt to record arithmetical computation	79
Description of Barbour machine	80
Barbour machine not practical	81
Description of Baldwin machine	82
Baldwin's printing mechanism	89
First key-set crank operated machine and first attempt to record the items in addition	90
Description of Pottin machine	91
Early efforts of Wm. S. Burroughs	95
General scheme of Burroughs' first inventions	96
Brief description of machine of early Burroughs' patents	97
All early arithmetical printing devices impractical	101
Practical method for recording disclosed later	102
Inoperative features of early recording mechanism	105
Adding mechanism attached to typewriter	105
Description of Ludlum machine	106
Ludlum machine inoperative	108

First Practical Recorders

Burroughs a bank clerk	111
Felt interested in recorder Art	111
Felt's first recording machine	113
Felt recording mechanism combined with his calculating machine	113

Ingram Content Group UK Ltd.
Milton Keynes UK
UKHW021816130323
418485UK00006B/506